Sin Comes of Age

BOOKS BY DUNCAN E. LITTLEFAIR

PUBLISHED BY THE WESTMINSTER PRESS

Sin Comes of Age

The Glory Within You:
Modern Man and the Spirit

Sin
Comes
of Age

by
Duncan E. Littlefair

THE WESTMINSTER PRESS
PHILADELPHIA

Scripture quotations from the Revised Standard Version of the Bible are copyright, 1946 and 1952, by the Division of Christian Education of the National Council of Churches, and are used by permission.

BOOK DESIGN BY DOROTHY E. JONES

PUBLISHED BY THE WESTMINSTER PRESS®
PHILADELPHIA, PENNSYLVANIA

PRINTED IN THE UNITED STATES OF AMERICA

———————

Acknowledgment is made to the following for permission to use copyrighted materials:

Harcourt Brace Jovanovich, Inc., for lines from "Little Gidding," "Four Quartets," T. S. Eliot, *Complete Poems and Plays* (Harcourt, Brace and Company, Inc., 1952).

Macmillan Publishing Co., Inc.; The Macmillan Company of Canada, Ltd. and Mrs. Iris Wise and Macmillan London and Basingstoke, Ltd., for lines from "The Twins," in James Stephens, *Collected Poems.* Copyright 1915 by Macmillan Publishing Co., Inc.; renewed 1943 by James Stephens.

———————

Library of Congress Cataloging in Publication Data

Littlefair, Duncan E   1912–
    Sin comes of age.

    Includes bibliographical references and index.
    1. Sin.   2. Good and evil.   3. Sins.
4. Salvation.   I. Title.
BV4625.L54   233'.2   75–23277
ISBN 0–664–20807–X

Good and Bad are in my heart;
But I cannot tell to you—
For they never are apart—
Which is the better of the two.
I am this! I am the other—
And the devil is my brother.
But my father, He is God!
And my mother is the Sod!
So I shelter love and hate
Like twin brothers in a nest.

—*James Stephens*

CONTENTS

FOREWORD

"All of us for whom the old gods have failed need to be lifted up into the light that will hold us by its spell and send us on refreshed by the vision in our souls." Such was the theme of the sermon at the Fountain Street Church in Grand Rapids, Michigan, on September 10, 1944.

Thus began the improbable ministry of Duncan Littlefair amidst a city noted for its religious conservatism—a ministry that has continued there for more than thirty years in a large and flourishing church. During all those years, Duncan Littlefair has appealed to thousands for whom the old gods had failed or, in the cases of the young, for whom the old gods could never succeed. He has lifted people, old and young, into the light of his brilliant sermons and has sent them on refreshed by a newly evoked vision in their souls.

Dr. Littlefair studied to become a minister at McMaster University in Canada—the country of his birth and youth—then at the University of Chicago, where he earned a doctorate of philosophy, and at universities in Germany and Switzerland. That he could find a sizable and receptive audience for the sermons he intended to preach was then an exceedingly remote prospect, according to contemporaries of his student days. But that first measure of his chances for ministerial employment proved to be a poor forecast of how this man was to build a long and remarkably successful ministry on:

Being skeptical of ideas said to be sacred and absolute but having faith in relationships known to be temporal and relative

Espousing no dogma as a solution to problems but seeking solutions through advancing fresh principles

Shunning the hope of supernatural grace but exalting the promise of human interaction

Regarding the stories about Jesus as myth but the teachings as gospel worth believing

Reading the Bible as ancient literature but its message as living truth

Speaking of God as a variable concept but of love as invariably God

The voice of Dr. Littlefair is commanding, but the command is that each person shall think for himself. The brilliance of his sermons derives not alone from his insights and vision but from the poetry and emphasis with which they are spoken. The effect of a sermon upon his congregation is always stimulating, often unsettling; and it rarely fails to enhance the spiritual growth of the listener.

Readers of this book based on thoughts and ideas originally expressed by Dr. Littlefair in his sermons may miss, I fear, some of the flavor and excitement that come from hearing him in person. And surely they will not have the same extraordinary source to sustain and encourage them as do members of his congregation and many other friends who, when troubled or grieved or bewildered, turn to him for uniquely helpful counseling. But those who first meet the author through this book will be rewarded in ways that shall set them apart from all who may miss the opportunity and that shall exalt them above all except those of us who have long known him as a dear, close, provocative, loving friend.

PHILIP BUCHEN
*Counsel to the President
of the United States*

Washington, D.C.

PREFACE

For more than thirty years Duncan E. Littlefair has been preaching at the Fountain Street Church in Grand Rapids, Michigan. His congregation typically ranges from 1,000 to 1,700 people. His more than 1,200 sermons to date have ranged from such subjects as the nature of God and the life of Jesus to marriage and sex, individual decision-making, and the pardon of former president Richard M. Nixon. He preaches without a manuscript, sometimes without even an outline, and he has never given all or part of the same sermon twice.

It may be, a local newspaperman once wrote, "the best Sunday show in Grand Rapids." There is no aspect of society, the establishment, or institutional Christianity that Littlefair has not questioned. His "Peck's bad boy" approach to religion has cost Fountain Street its longtime membership in the Baptist Association, and his audacious criticisms of business, government, education, the media, the military, and parents have sent many parishioners out in a huff, some never to return to the fold. Still people keep pouring in, bustling and convivial before the service starts, rapt and attentive as it progresses. Often a kind of tension grows over the gathering, like the strained atmosphere before an electrical storm. On more than one occasion the mood has ignited, producing an explosion of applause at the end of the sermon.

How could such an approach succeed in a conservative, traditional, affluent Midwestern city? People have been pondering that question for years. Journalist Robert Sherrill, writing in *The New York Times Magazine* in October 1974, considered the "maverick Fountain Street Church" to be a conundrum no outsider could hope to explain. An insider, writing in *The Grand Rapids Press,* has attributed much of Littlefair's success to his preaching style. "It's the voice. The volume can be a bellow or a whisper, the tone strident or soothing or pleading. And the gestures. Hands cupped; held high; always roaming." Apparently Littlefair had this ability back in the early 1940's when he began his preaching career at the Kenilworth Union Church near Chicago. "During my graduate years at the University of Chicago," recalls Huston Smith, celebrated author of several books on religious philosophy, "I would rise at dawn and ride for two hours to hear this silver-tongued orator."

Some observers feel that the influential congregation is a drawing card. "Top officials of both Democratic and Republican parties are members," *The New York Times Magazine* article noted, "so are labor executives and some of the most entrenched capitalists of Grand Rapids, as well as some editors and reporters." Other observers attribute part of Littlefair's appeal to the national publicity he has gained in magazines such as *Time* and from appearances on television. His interview with the late Frank McGee on the *Today Show* in 1973 generated an unprecedented response from all across the nation.

It is also reported that Littlefair's reputation as a prophet of social change lures many people. "I don't agree with a lot of what he says," a Grand Rapids businessman confided to me, "but I'll say this: his ability as a forecaster is absolutely uncanny." The black power movement in the 1960's, the student revolt against the educational establishment, the massive Vietnam war tragedy, the currently budding challenge to such venerable American values as competition and private property—these are among the many developments he foresaw years before they became news.

Valid as they may be, explanations like these do not tell the story. Littlefair's preaching style is surely an asset, but many hundreds of lesser-known preachers have developed unusual speaking skills too. The influential congregation is also a plus, but neighboring churches (such as the one that President Gerald R. Ford attends when he is home) have their share of the city's notables. Publicity may have had some effect, but it has come after the fact rather than before it; Fountain Street's great church house was filled twenty-five years before the national media discovered Littlefair. As for his talents of prediction, though they are impressive he is no Merlin and does not pretend to have a crystal ball.

When the University of Chicago awarded Littlefair its Alumni Citation for "creative citizenship and exemplary leadership" in 1970, one of the nominating statements cited described his approach as "rich with love, warmth, faith, and hope." If there is one key to his success, this may be it. Intellectual, analytical, and critical his ideas may be, but the message begins and ends with a deep, poignant, intensely reverent affection for life—not just the "good" life but all life, whatever its forms, frailties, aberrations, and idiosyncrasies. "If it moves," I once heard someone say, "he loves it." His denunciations of wrongdoing can be hard, but always he hugs the wrong*doer.* Sin, in his view, is an expression of the spirit. This approach gives him a remarkable capacity to help people see what their lives are all about.

In turn, Littlefair finds the congregation a source of inspiration. As many observers have noted, it bursts with creativity—an elegant music program, an exciting church school, imaginative arts and crafts projects, innovative study groups, and numerous other centers of initiative. The congregation has its conflicts and stresses, to be sure, but withal there is an extraordinary sense of community, sharing, and enthusiasm. "You can't give the spirit away," Littlefair has said over and over again. "The more you give, the more you get back." The congregation's response could be one of his proofs. Certainly it has added depth, dimension, and color to his approach.

Littlefair's last book, *The Glory Within You* (The Westminster Press, 1973), concerned the spirit. This book, his third, goes to the other end of the religious spectrum and deals with sin. Despite their difference in emphasis, both books reflect the same basic philosophy; in fact, as emphasized in the opening chapter, Littlefair sees good and evil as part and parcel of the same spiritual whole.

This book was suggested in the spring of 1974 by Philip W. Buchen, then a Grand Rapids attorney and chairman of the Duncan E. Littlefair Fund, now serving as chief legal counsel to the President of the United States. Buchen believed that Littlefair's recently completed series of sermons on sin could be the basis for a relevant, helpful, and provocative book.

After a short introduction to the nature of sin and

evil in modern society, therefore, this book focuses on seven deadly sins today. By focusing on these sins, Littlefair does not exclude other attitudes and tendencies that also may be described as sinful. His seven are picked on the basis of an unusually well demonstrated capacity to threaten love, life, and creativity as we know it. In the last three chapters Littlefair presents ideas about how to deal with sin in contemporary life.

This book has been pieced together from a multitude of transcripts of sermons, talks, notes, and other materials produced by Littlefair. For the substantive views expressed, he alone is responsible, though for failures of clarity and coherence I must share the blame as editor. My work in helping to prepare the manuscript was underwritten by the Duncan E. Littlefair Fund of Fountain Street Church, which also underwrote the preparation of *The Glory Within You.* The Extension Service of the church again provided the printed transcripts of the sermons we used.

The Biblical references are from the Revised Standard Version of the Bible.

The author and I are grateful to the staff and many members of Fountain Street Church for their encouragement and help. We owe special thanks to Marian U. Kirchner and Patricia J. Suhorsky for preparing the manuscript for publication and handling numerous secretarial duties. Rebecca and Betsy Ewing did most of the work of preparing the index.

DAVID W. EWING

Part I

THE EVIL
THAT MEN DO

CHAPTER 1

The Devil
Is My Brother

We live in what is called a scientific age, and science is characterized by its classification of information. Wherever a scientific approach is found, delineations can be found—categories, subcategories, precise identifications, and so forth. The more scientific a program, the more rigidly defined are the pieces of information used. The scientific approach teaches us to separate in order to be logical. It helps us to put facts and deductions in relationship to one another. It helps us to distinguish one thing from another so we do not become confused.

So we classify animals, people, chemical elements, space, time, dangers, religions, and political ideas. We draw charts of organizations to show how people in departments and committees are separated but relate to one another and to the head. We distinguish between dark and light and night and day. We make it clear that "yes" is the opposite of "no."

We take a similar approach to good and evil. We call them different categories of being. When we say "This is good" we mean it is not evil; evil is something over there on the other side of this thing called good.

But while this approach is essential to logic, it does not describe nature. In nature there are no sharp distinctions and straight lines. In textbooks and discussion we may *impose* such classifications for the sake of communication, but they are artificial and unreal. For example, in nature it is not clear where animal and human life divide. One flows into the other. Nor is it clear at all where the mind stops and the body begins; it seems more accurate to state that mind *is* body, despite the fact that the words connote discrete qualities. It is not even clear where life and nonlife are divided. Lewis Mumford points out that the absence of life or life potentiality is an illusion. " 'Matter' has in the constitution and most intimate structure of certain elements that which is capable, at some far point in its own evolution, of fulfilling its potentiality for becoming 'alive.' "[1]

Thus, our attempts to clarify nature by making distinctions lead to perversions of reality. The separations may be useful for practical projects, but they have an enormous potential for damage when they produce untrue pictures of our world. This is why the expert uses his terms with great care. When he (or she) says "yes," he always includes some degree of "no." When he talks about one part of the body, he is aware that part includes other sections and cannot truly be separated from them except in thought.

I suggest that the symbol of the Yin and Yang is a truer representation of life and nature than scientific schemata are. This symbol, from the ancient Chinese, is a circle with black and white forms inside.[2] As you look at the symbol, the white and black *together* make the total circle. The white form could not exist without the black, and vice versa. To put it another way, when you make the white form, you outline the black form; and they are drawn so that they move in and out of each other, somewhat like pieces of a jigsaw puzzle.

In the early periods of human history, people knew there were no radical differences in life. They also knew that they had to make distinctions for the sake of communication, so in China the Yin and Yang symbol was developed to show the wholeness and roundedness of life. To emphasize the meaning further, they put a black circle in the middle of the white part, and a white circle in the black, thus dramatizing that the two are inseparable and have to be understood together.

This symbol represents the reality of life and nature. Supposed opposites like mind and body, animal and man, night and day, yes and no, are not radically separated but belong to each other. Further, they create each other. There is no night without day. There is no mind without body. There is no life without death. There is no matter without antimatter. There is no creation without destruction.

The traditional representation of evil is a very good illustration of our desire to distinguish, clarify, and simplify so that we can see quickly. How have we dramatized evil? We invented the devil. He is red, has horns, holds a pitchfork, has a tail. How could you mistake him? Centuries ago he was created in this obvious form so no one would confuse him with God. The inventors of the devil wanted to make it clear that he was outside of us. We didn't have horns or a tail; therefore we stood apart from him. He was an objective enemy—to be fought with the help of God, who was on our side. It was hoped that one day we would win a clear-cut victory over him.

Now, we may not personify the struggle today in such graphic terms, but we think of good and evil as separate. The devil and evil are "out there" somewhere, in our minds. "Out there" may be closer for some than for others, but it is a distinct place. Therefore the devil can be driven out of the world someday. This assumption permeates much of our thinking about personal goals and social ideals. It underlies many of our proverbs and dictums, such as "See no evil, hear no evil, speak no evil."

But the devil is not "out there" in fact. And there is no such thing or person as the devil, to the best of our knowledge. However, there is great evil in the world. I believe there always will be, just as there always has been evil in the past. The more we learn about good, the more we learn about evil, for evil is part of the good, wherever it is found. I believe we will never be able to separate one clearly from the other.

Many close observers of human nature agree on this basic observation. In the quotation at the beginning of this book, the fine Irish poet, James Stephens, writes that "the devil is my brother. But my father, He is God! And my mother is the Sod!"[3] Fyodor Dostoevsky, in his novel *The Idiot,* provides this remarkable insight:

> The law of self-destruction and the law of self-preservation are equally strong in humanity! The devil has equal dominion over humanity till the limit of time which we know not. You laugh? You don't believe in the devil? Disbelief in the devil is a French idea, a frivolous idea. Do you know who the devil is? Do you know his name? Without even knowing his name you laugh at the form of him, following Voltaire's example, at his hoofs, at his tail, at his horns, which you have invented; for the devil is a mighty menacing spirit, but he has not the hoofs and horns you've invented for him.[4]

And here is a statement from the writings of Sigmund Freud:

> We humans carry within us the seeds of our own destruction and we nourish them continuously. We must hate as well as love. We *will* to destroy ourselves and our fellowman, as well as to create and protect them.[5]

Jesus seemed well aware that it is exceedingly difficult to tell God from the devil:

> Then if any one says to you, "Lo, here is the Christ!" or "There he is!" do not believe it. For false Christs and false prophets will arise and show great signs and wonders, so as to lead astray, if possible, even the elect. Lo, I have told you beforehand. So, if they say to you, "Lo, he is in the wilderness," do not go out; if they say, "Lo, he is in the inner rooms," do not believe it. (Matt. 24:23–26.)

Christianity could not have been the continuing, dynamic religion it has been for nearly two thousand years without having many essential truths, and one of them is the inseparability of sin from human nature. Sin as the Christian church defined it is a narrower concept than the one I shall use in subsequent chapters, but that difference does not matter here. Regardless of its theological refinements, varying superstructures, elaborate hierarchies, and varying applications by churches, Christianity has spoken to the heart of man. It has said, in effect: "You are born in sin. You are a sinner in your heart. Don't separate yourself in your piety from the evil and the wicked, because you *are* the evil and the wicked. You belong to them. Indeed, you make them." No Christian who really believes in his religion can get away from this self-condemnation. Evil is not some fanciful demon that you can be sure of identifying. In fact, when you think you are serving God you *may* in fact be serving the devil. You are never sure when you are doing what.

The myth that Christianity has used to dramatize good and evil—God versus Satan, heaven versus hell—may no longer be a satisfactory one. For many of us, it is an assault on the senses, and so we have moved away from it. We have gone beyond the notion of a world in which a devil could be a being as well as God. We have lost something in so doing. Man at his most glorious, saintly best is still an animal—and at his best he *knows* he is an animal. In our desire for perfection we may think we have got to be perfect, but in our most thoughtful and aware moments there can be no confusion about the importance of the animal in us.

If we reject the myth of the devil, we must find a more valid, more relevant one (I use the term "myth" to refer to a means of relating truth in picturesque forms, or describing events that could be real but are imagined). We must find a new way of seeing evil—our inadequacies, imperfections, faults, sinfulness. We must find a new way to recognize our involvement with people who are less than they ought to be, perhaps because of failures of omission or commission on our part. We must find more appropriate ways of relating the worst of us to the best and the fortunate to the unfortunate so that we do not shatter our communities. In short, we must become more aware, more understanding. We must be able to see the death in life, the joy in suffering, the failure in victory, the evil in good. Otherwise we cannot be alert to these realities so as to manage and direct our activities effectively. This is the kind of awareness that Jesus tried to create by his condemnation of the churches and the good people.

In his book *Love and Will,* Rollo May notes that not to see the demonic is to make the demonic.[6] I believe it is very important to know our enemies. If we don't know them, we won't stop them; in giving them anonymity, we give them a chance to become even more destructive than otherwise they would be. May gives an illustration that struck home with me. It was the desire of the people in the United Kingdom and the United States to escape from the grossness of the picture of the devil, he says, that rendered them incapable of recognizing the evil of Hitler in the 1930's. We could not believe that a human being could do what reportedly he was doing. I remember sitting in a church in Toronto in 1936 listening to a Jewish rabbi talk about the coffins that came back sealed after relatives had disappeared in the dead of the night. And I thought: "It can't be true. No one could do that!" We were blinded by our own aspirations and ideals.

Let me try to put some of the preceding thoughts into the form of maxims:

The only way to enhance the good in our lives is to see the evil.

The only way to know the meaning of love is to know some of the hate and resentment harbored within us.

The only way to be totally human is to recognize that we are animals.

If we find our wholeness, we will develop a humility that will bring us closer to others, and we will acquire strength and compassion.

When we find these qualities, we will increase our power to make the world we live in a more peaceful, more creative, and happier place.

Recognizing Evil

How are we to recognize evil? It can be an attractive force. If it were obviously bad, who would choose it? Only in grotesque movies or plays of exaggeration for children is the devil clearly wicked. In real life he comes to be welcomed. He may be friendly, open, honest, attractive—and he makes attractive propositions. This is why he is so prominent in our myths and legends. For instance, in the Biblical story of Jesus' temptation after fasting in the wilderness, the devil offered the kingdoms of the world at an attractive and sensible price. If Jesus was hungry, what could be more reasonable than turning stones into bread to eat? If Jesus wanted to prove to people that he represented the kingdom, what could be more sensible than to demonstrate it by throwing himself from the pinnacle of the Temple and being rescued by angels? There was nothing sinister in the devil's manner or propositions.

Albert Speer, the Nazi war criminal who was released in 1968 after twenty years of imprisonment in Spandau, once stated that "you do not feel the devil when first he puts his hand upon your shoulder." Speer referred to the appeal of Hitler, who, if he had been obviously evil, could not have been so successful. Hitler would bring the German people peace and order. He would stop the quarreling in the streets, get rid of the rowdies, take the beggars off the corners. He would put bread in the mouths of the hungry. He would rouse the once-great nation from its lethargy and make it a leading power in the world. And he had a plan for doing these things that would work—and did, for a while. Under Hitler, people who had been beaten and broken became alive and vital. The sounds of crying in the ashes were transformed into the steps of young men marching in the streets with shovels on their shoulders to rebuild the Fatherland. So when Hitler asked Speer to construct a building for him, why should Speer have refused? Not until a long time thereafter did Speer realize that he had accepted the hand of the devil.

Many years ago I read the story of a professor of international law at the University of Vienna. During his stay in a Nazi concentration camp he was put in charge of feeding the pigs. When some of his fellow prisoners tried to steal some of the slop he was feeding the pigs, he informed on them. When he was brought to trial, after the war, he was crazed and demented. Yet from the dim recesses of his mind he pulled a profound quotation from the famous Roman writer, Juvenal. "The depths of depravity," the professor reminded the court, "are not reached in one step."[7]

We don't feel the devil when he puts his hand on our shoulder, nor do we go the route with him in one step —but that is not all of the problem. Compounding the difficulty of recognition is that what we have known as good can *become* evil. The creative force or principle we once held may turn destructive as we hold it. Conversely, what was evil can become good, or potentially good, so that it deserves watching and nurturing. This is the nature of good and evil in an organic life, where forces do not stay set in fixed categories but are continually changing and flowing into one another. Let us consider some everyday examples:

Innocence is a quality of goodness, most of us would agree. It is good to be clean and free and unburdened by malevolent intentions, efforts to mislead others, and pretenses to conceal the truth. But are all kinds of innocence good, and at all times? The pristine form just described could not stand in front of Hitler. It would not be helpful in many negotiations with militant dictatorships. It might not hold up in law enforcement work against the underworld. In other words, there are times when innocence is ignorance and liable to be destructive.

Unselfishness is a quality that people treasure in their highest hopes and ideals, and rightly so. But this quality, too, is protean. Unselfishness may put too much of a burden on someone else, as when an idealistic family breadwinner forgoes income his family requires. On the other hand, it may relieve other people of burdens they should carry, as when one family member takes on too much of the worrying. It may also be a way of avoiding responsibility (if you don't take your share of the kitty, you don't have to worry about spending it wisely). It may even be a way of making yourself so attractive to others that you can proceed to manipulate them ("I am a fine and good person, therefore you should cooperate with me").

Peacefulness is a quality that the world must have in order to survive—who would disagree with this? Yet it does not take too much experience to learn that a peaceful posture is not always a virtue. Can the resistance movements in Poland, Czechoslovakia, and other countries overrun by the Nazis be faulted for their efforts to sabotage and upset their unwanted rulers? Would an idealistic, unilateral program of U.S. disarmament be likely to end tensions in a world where there are ugly, brutal, materialistic powers to contend with?

In sum, the devil may present himself to us in attractive ways. His price may seem fair. He asks only that we take one step or make one concession. The quality or activity he urges on us may have an aura of goodness about it because of its use last month or last year. It should be no wonder, therefore, that we see much of him in American life.

An illustration? Let's take demonstrations. When Martin Luther King, Jr., and fellow leaders organized the demonstrations for black people's rights, in the 1950's and 1960's, they planned with wisdom and genius. In effect, they were saying to the world: "Do you know what goes on in some of these U.S. states? What happens there is against the Constitution and other laws, but no one does anything about it. Do Americans know how the dignity of man is being violated in their country?" The demonstrations were effective, capturing national attention, inducing Washington to enforce statutes never before enforced and leading legislatures to make changes in the law.

Then militant students borrowed the demonstration technique in the late 1960's to produce change on the campuses. No one stopped to question their tactics. The technique had worked well for the black nonviolence movement, had it not? The universities were in need of reform, were they not? So educational administrators gave in to the demonstrators on one campus after another. The few administrators who opposed the students were condemned—they were blocking reform, they were like the white supremacists in the South! Campus demonstrations worked so well, in fact, that many universities became places where people did not sit down to reason together but rather imposed or acceded to demands and ultimatums. The student-administration meetings were not held for the raising of questions and the pursuit of explanations. While it was encouraging that students refused to accede to university heads taking an "I don't care whether they protest, I don't care how they feel" attitude, there was reason to ask if the good bought in this way was not destructive and perhaps not worth the price.

The insurgents took another step; as the Viennese law professor said, they did not reach the depths all at once. They began refusing to listen to spokesmen for the opposition. Then another step: refusing to allow opponents to speak at all, with the threat of clubs, stones, and guns. It did not take much foresight to see that if they were going to assert themselves in this way, it would not be long before opposition groups counter-moved with similar tactics, and indeed that is what took place.

During this period I happened to attend a seminar at the University of Michigan. There an upperclass-man told me that student protesters were going to abol-ish R.O.T.C. I asked why. He answered, "Because we don't like it." I asked, "Why don't you like it?" He said, "Because it's immoral." I asked, "Who determined that?" He answered, "We determined it." I told him: "Well, has it occurred to you that I may not like athlet-ics? [I do, but I wanted an example to drive my point home to him.] It shouldn't take much wisdom to realize that if you abolish R.O.T.C. because you don't like it, somebody else is going to abolish athletics because they don't like them, or maybe some research program being undertaken by the university. If you establish this way of operating, it will be used against you; if you set this standard, you will have to subject yourself to it later. So I wonder if abolishing R.O.T.C. as you're doing is worth the price you will pay."

I suggest three tests for recognizing the hand of the devil:

1. In your mind, universalize the activity, process, or principle you would adopt. How would it feel if those who bore you ill will had the power to use the method you would use? Would it be a reasonably good way for people everywhere to act?

2. Consider whether the approach you are consider-ing would shut out anyone or restrict some group arbi-

trarily. Would it shut out the blacks? Would it curtail a rival group or competitor? Would it restrict the socialists or communists? Would it put the Aryans in their place? You may despise what they are or stand for, but if your approach cuts down one group in particular, it is not good. In this organic life of ours, we cannot hurt one part without hurting the whole.

3. Ask if the course you would take would sacrifice the future for the present. This great bang you get out of drugs, this violation of the pollution law you can get away with scot-free for the time being, this fling you can enjoy to the fullest—are you buying for the present at too great a cost to the future? As I once heard novelist Norman Mailer put it: "You may mortgage your future too much because that experience you have may be bought at too great a price. You may be borrowing too much from God."

CHAPTER 2

What Is Sin?

Sin is associated with condemnation and guilt. It is an oppressive concept for most people. Even those of us who have not been brought up in a traditional religion have experienced a sense of guilt due to sin, a feeling that somehow or other we have offended God and will be punished. As a child I pictured a gigantic figure surrounded by lightning flashes—God pointing the finger of condemnation at someone who had offended him. Sometimes I picture an evangelist whipping up fear in his congregation so the members will come to the altar for relief from sin. Such notions of sin are burdensome, and even though they have become increasingly unacceptable, they have caused and continue to cause a great deal of harm.

Sin is a changeable concept. The classical list of the seven deadly sins (that is, serious sins requiring formal ecclesiastical penance to save the sinner from eternal damnation, as opposed to venial sins, which can be forgiven through prayer and fasting) was begun in the fifth century. But even then the list did not stay the same. Various authorities took the privilege of changing the sins according to their personal judgments. Nor did the list always stay at seven, a number chosen because of its mystical importance in those days. Other sins were added at various times. The generally accepted list of seven deadly sins was compiled by Gregory the Great. The sins were pride, envy, anger, sloth, avarice, gluttony, and lust. Sometimes lust was described as unchastity. Other sins occasionally substituted were gloominess or dejection and languid indifference. The sins listed were generally those of the flesh, of daily physical excess—what might be called external sins as opposed to internal, or spiritual, sins.

Sins have been qualified in different ways. "Thou shalt not kill" is one of the best known of the Ten Commandments. But capital punishment is legal in many states, and some types of homicide are considered justifiable. For the Jewish people in Biblical times, the commandment was more restricted still. Samuel, the high priest of the Jewish people, berated Saul for not killing King Agag after defeating Agag's forces. Then Samuel called the defeated king in front of him. Chained and manacled, Agag came in, according to the Scripture, "with glory in his heart," because he felt that now the killing was over and he would be able to go back to his people. But the high priest took his sword and slashed the chained king to pieces. We know also from the Scriptures that the Jews were sometimes ordered by their God to go out and kill without mercy—not merely their enemies but their enemies' livestock as well, not merely the males but also women and children.

It is interesting to note what has *not* passed as sin. Until twenty or so years ago, war was deemed as being within the grace of God. Only after World War I did a religious movement grow to condemn war as sinful.

Up to and including the present, the leaders of many Christian churches have blessed the instruments of war.

Today we think of slavery as sinful, but for hundreds of years good Christian people basked in the privileges of slavery and agreed it was the will of God that some should be slaves.

As late as the nineteenth century, Christians could watch and support the hanging of nine- and ten-year-old children for petty thefts, including stealing food in order to keep themselves and their families alive. Until a few decades ago, pious Christians enjoyed the benefits of child labor. They went to church to confess their sins, but their sins did not include conscripting children for work in unsafe and inhumane conditions.

The degradation of women was not considered a sin until the present century. A husband owned his wife—had full legal and physical control, in the eyes of the church. He owned his children, too.

The dreadful condition of many jails, hospitals, and insane asylums is not considered a sin. The public humiliation of a person, done with joy and satisfaction, is on no official list of sins today. We are only beginning to think of the destruction of the environment—endangered animal species as well as energy resources and beauty—as sinful.

Now turn to some of the acts that *have* been deemed sinful. An old friend of mine tells me that when he went to a small, well-regarded college in Michigan he had to sign an article stating that he would not play "devil cards," go to the movies, or dance. In the eyes of the great church that governed that college, those activities were (and are) serious sins. Again, wearing pretty clothes or decorations has been a sin in some Christian communities. Not going to church has been considered sinful, as well as not going to confess sins.

And, of course, throughout Western history we have been preoccupied with the many sins associated with thoughts and acts of sex.

Surely something has been askew in our interpretation of sin. How could we have condoned so many horrible, destructive acts while we condemned so many enjoyable, normally trivial activities? What we need is a concept of sin that is both more useful and realistic —and therefore more acceptable—and more religious in the broad sense of the word. We need a concept more relevant to the ways we relate ourselves to society and the world. I want to offer such a concept now.

Let us define sin as an offense against God. Let us define it further as an offense that is measurable, demonstrable, and determinable in a factual, empirical way. Let us rule out sins that are determined by whim or sacred authority without evidence that the offense is really destructive. If we are going to make ourselves responsible for sin, we are going to have to demonstrate that the evil in our society is truly evil; we are going to have to make the case convincing to the finest, best, most rigorous scientific minds.

We can sin against our fellowman. We can sin against ourselves. We can sin against the institutions of society. We can sin against nature. But always the sin must be *through* our actions and *against* God. Whatever interferes with God is a sin.

What is God? I define God as the most important force or presence we know about and can experience. Therefore God is that power in our universe which is most significant, most fundamental, most necessary to the development of man. In a word, God is creativity. He is found wherever creativity is found, wherever anything new is emerging, wherever people are being related in new ways and at new levels. He is found at birth, in friendship, in love, in innovation, in artistic effort, in acts of courage, and in countless other aspects of our growing life.

To define sin more precisely, let us call it any act whatsoever that interferes with the creativity of life, any act that interferes with love and the opening up of our individual, family, or collective corporate life. Let sin be any act that impedes our growth in understanding and depth of appreciation of human relationships; anything that blocks the development of a richer life for man; anything that interferes with the evolutionary process toward a greater, nobler, more joyous humanity.

Given this definition, it is obvious there is much in our society that is sinful. In this book I presume to name seven deadly sins, but there may be many more. They are all extremely important to us, for by definition they threaten our continued existence as a species.

To understand the precise nature of sin, we need to know what it is *not.* Let me describe briefly some notions or representations of sin that strike me as false and misleading.

First, sin is *not* a separation from God. Many people, it seems to me, have the conviction that when they sin they have been somehow cut off from God. It is easy to understand that acts of hampering or restricting the goodness of God could lead to the feeling of being at odds with him, but that is not the same thing as being shut off from him. No sin or series of sins could possibly shut off even the worst of persons from the goodness of God, as he is defined here. If God is creativity producing life, then surely he is at work in every human. It is impossible to be human and be separated from God. No matter how badly a person may have sinned, he or she lives and moves in God and cannot lose him.

Second, sin is *not* a personal affront to God. Large

numbers of Christians feel, deep down inside as a result of early training, that a sin is a kind of insult to God, as though he were a person like themselves who could take umbrage at some mistake or lack of concern. This notion stems from the ancient concept of God as a supreme monarch who watches over what we do. As I have pointed out earlier, this belief has become unacceptable to most Americans. What evidence is there to justify the conclusion that God looks after individuals or behaves like a person?

Many traditional sins are in the realm of lese majesty. We do not speak to God properly. We do not begin our prayers with the proper words. We must not be too forward with God. We must not argue with him, as Job did. We must not say things about him that he wouldn't like. I venture to suggest that in many cities and towns such offenses would be recognized more quickly as sins than any other acts, with the exceptions of murder and adultery.

Third, there is *not* such a thing as an unpardonable sin. In our traditional theology, there was a hierarchy of sins: some minor ones that did not disturb God very much, and some gross ones that disturbed him severely. And there was one unpardonable sin which God found it impossible to forgive. Jesus called it blasphemy against the Holy Spirit. But in the philosophy that I present in this volume, there can be no place for an unpardonable sin. Such a notion is inconsistent with the loving nature of Jesus and with the Gospels themselves. It has no place in a philosophy that understands God as a creative power working within every human being. In fact, it has no place in any religion that accepts God as the supremely loving spirit.

Fourth, sins can *not* be identified and categorized for all time. I am aware that this statement flies in the face of a strongly entrenched notion. There has been an illusion of permanence about the Ten Commandments, the Sermon on the Mount, and the pronouncements of Jesus and the various prophets. There is the venerable tradition that the church has it within its power to write books listing those acts which constitute sin. But surely it ought to be clear to us that it is utterly impossible to make a list of sins that could stand for all time and all places. We know that morality changes from generation to generation and culture to culture. We know that our understanding of the nature of life can deepen. We know that the conditions of life and work change, creating different needs and dangers. For example, in the age of feudalism usury was counted as one of the greatest of sins. But with the advent of capitalism and the necessity of moneylending, interest charges became a necessity of industrial growth. So what had been a sin became a high virtue, even in the Calvinistic society of western Europe.

Fifth, sin is *not* always the opposite of what is good and virtuous. If we identify a sin and then determine its opposite virtue, it is probable that we can conceive of circumstances under which the opposite virtue is a sin, perhaps a more grievous one than the first. For example, suppose we name hate as a sin. Is love, then, always a virtue? I suspect most readers can remember an occasion in their lives when love was a hampering, frustrating restriction, not a means of enlarging and enriching their lives. In my counseling work I have come across many such instances. For a well-known example, consider the life of Helen Keller. In her early years her family was so gentle, so tender, so kind to her that they almost killed her with affection. Again, anyone who has worked with crippled or handicapped persons knows that tenderness can have a different meaning to the receiver from that intended by the giver.

Suppose you name arrogance as a sin. The opposite would be the virtue of humility. Is humility always good? Even humility in the face of God can be corrosive. All the great saints have readily acknowledged this—it was part of the agony they suffered. For the more they humbled themselves, the more pride they took in their humility, with the result that they felt farther away from God.

My point is not that we should be cynical of virtue, only that life is not so simple that we can say categorically, This you should do and this you should not do. I am aware that a clear, positive list of sins gives many people assurance and confidence—we would all like to feel wise enough to write rules in marble for ourselves and others. This feeling helps us to build big and successful churches that appeal to people who are worried and in doubt. But surely the infinite goodness of God gives us cause to think about our limitations, and we have good reason to feel uneasy when we try to decide exactly what would best promote the goodness of God.

Having looked at what sin is not, let us turn to some of the basic characteristics of sinfulness. I submit the following propositions:

1. *Sinfulness is self-consciousness.* Those trained in traditional religious approaches will immediately recognize the doctrine of original sin as the basis for this statement. For a growing number of people today, that doctrine is a myth, but it is a beautiful myth and it is psychologically sound. When Adam ate of the tree of knowledge, he became aware—of himself, of his capacity to think, of his ability to decide. From that time forward, man had to be insecure, for he was no longer an unconscious part of the universe. He was a co-worker with God, seeking to understand God and obliged for his own salvation to learn and try to under-

stand so that he might come to God on his own. Unlike
the animals, he was no longer just operating and being
operated on as an organism. Now he could say "no" to
God, "no" to any proposition or project, good or bad.

What was more, man was separated from himself as
well as from the universe that nourished him. He was
divided between the impulses that came from his biological inheritance (especially his subconscious) and
those that came from his conscious mind. He became
torn between different desires, torn between instinc-
tive compulsions and rational ideals, torn between
different ways of deciding. This split in human nature
has been obvious through all of recorded history. A
person's very desire to know comes between him (or
her) and God. The person wills to protect himself and
live, but as soon as he becomes conscious of himself, he
puts a kind of barrier between himself and God. For
now he is concerned not with the growth of the goodness of God but with his own particular desires. Does
he serve himself or does he serve God? Does he pursue
his individualistic desires or lose himself in the group?
He cannot meet another human being without sensing
a chasm between himself and the other.

Some Eastern religions solve this problem by elimi-
nating selfhood and trying to eliminate the individual,
but in the West this approach is not palatable; the dignity of the individual is cherished.

2. *Inertia is a leading source of sin.* Physical laws
describe how inertia works. Everything tends to run
down, to seek the lowest possible level of operation. So
it is with you and me. We don't go seeking possibilities
every day; we don't make a habit of seeking adventure
except when we're driven to it. We try to close in, to get
back into that womb from which knowledge has deliv-
ered us and where all is comfort and there are no deci-

sions to make. If God be creativity, inertia must be at the root of sinfulness.

3. *Partiality and specialization produce sin.* Anytime we concentrate on some given part of our life or some particular quality of ourselves, such as learning capacity or dexterity, we interfere with the creative interrelatedness of life. God operates to make wholes, not parts. So the more we work to achieve some one skill or ambition, the more we have to shut out the possibilities for developing other interests and needs of our personalities. Therefore we shut out God.

4. *Irresponsibility makes us sinful.* In that beautiful story about original sin, Adam blamed his wife for taking the apple—but not only his wife. Something at the subhuman level had to be held responsible, too, so the snake, representative of primordial life, was blamed. We have gone on blaming our errors on others ever since, forgetful of the ties that bind all people to one another. No matter what others have done to us, no matter what the conditions of our life may be, no matter how limited our inheritances, the fact is that we are responsible for what we do with what we have been given. Nobody *makes* us decide this or that, nor do we ever *have* to make this election or that. The only thing we have to do in our whole lives is die.

There are two profound implications of the characteristics described. Though they will be discussed in detail in later sections of this volume, it will be helpful to point them out now.

First, we should appreciate that sin is basic to human nature and inseparable from life. Indeed, as suggested, the highest values we know are connected with and involved in sin. A sinful act is not necessarily done consciously or in rebellion. The mistaken idea that all sin is avoidable was convenient for meting out punishment in primitive times, but it does not serve us well today.

If this is true—and it can be established beyond doubt with evidence from every area of society—then why must we go about carrying on our shoulders and in our hearts such overwhelming burdens of guilt? Why must we cry, bemoan, and lament our sinful natures? We are responsible for our sins, yes, but can we manage that responsibility better through feelings of guilt?

Second, we need loving communities to help us deal with our sins. We need to live among people who see themselves as they are, are willing to take us as we are, and have respect and appreciation for the glory of human nature with all its faults. There is no supernatural God to write "forgiven" in a book after we commit sins and feel sorry. Not on the trumpets of a storm or coming out of the mystery of fires will we find forgiveness. If we are to find forgiveness, we must turn to loving communities where the scars can disappear, where the cuts inflicted can heal over, where the barriers we place between us can give way to redeeming love.

Given the basic definition presented at the beginning of this chapter, I think sin is also a way of saying that somehow or other we have not done as well as we might have done in our friendships, family relationships, and community relationships. It is a way of saying that we have made a mistake, have failed. It is a profession of hope: we have not reached the desired point yet, but we are not complacent and will keep trying. When we say, "I have fallen short," we could use the term "sin" instead. In this sense, sin has a lengthy history—people questing for a better life but realizing their inadequacies, not feeling destroyed by them, knowing they could overcome their sins, realizing there was a process that would help them to do that. The process has always been love.

CHAPTER 3

The Vice of Virtue

Virtue is a constantly changing quality. It can never be finally, firmly settled. No person can ever be assured of his or her virtue because he or she has seen the light, accepted a code, made a commitment to the community or nation, or for any other reason. That which is thoroughly good now from a person's standpoint may tomorrow become something evil and destructive. That which was not good yesterday may, in the mystery of social change and growth, be good today. We cannot settle down in our convictions of virtue, quality, and goodness.

Thus virtue is an aspect of one of the main themes in this book: that no single action is always and everywhere good or evil. A good intention may issue in evil results; it is not necessarily, therefore, a good action. An evil intention may issue in good results; it is not necessarily, therefore, a bad act.

Those who think they are good are almost invariably not so. Jesus condemned such people. Virtually all the great spiritual leaders have known that when goodness becomes entrenched and recognized it ceases to be goodness, for those who think they are good shut themselves off from the fountain of the spirit. They are the Pharisees and hypocrites Jesus criticized.

The really good people are not sure of their goodness. Like Jesus, they ask, "Why do you call me good?" They are unsure about virtue, they struggle with the intricacies of their problems, they recognize that evil lurks within them and their heroes.

A person who thinks of himself (or herself) as truly virtuous raises a screen of arrogance between himself and others—arrogance that may masquerade as self-abnegating humility or piety but is a closed-mind determination to show that his intentions and actions are right. At the same time, though, he dislikes himself. He has trouble accepting his dark sides—his selfishness, venality, irrational passions. So he tries to shut out what he does not care for and to present himself as a model of goodness.

Now guilt enters the picture. It is my observation that the person who thinks of himself as virtuous is a guilt-ridden person. You or I may be able to shut out our evil tendencies from our consciousness, but we cannot shut them out of our behavior or basic knowledge. Subconsciously, if not consciously, we are aware deep down of the improper means by which we attempt sometimes to find our way through the jungle. When we try to hide the fact, we begin to feel guilty. Aware that we are not really as virtuous as we claim to be, we must live with the nagging worry that the evil in us will be seen by others despite our protestations of virtue. A chain effect develops that may render us unfit for our family, friends, work associates, and society.

Unpleasantness is another concomitant of virtuousness. When we show ourselves as very good people, our virtue becomes a load to carry. In our misery we become irritable and take it out on others. To put this thought in another way, nature has a way of taking its toll, as physicians and psychiatrists know. If we abuse our bodies, they rebel sooner or later and make us pay. Similarly, if we abuse our spirits, we end up paying a price. We begin picking at ourselves and others under the strain of trying to maintain the artificial world we have painted.

In his biography, the great psychiatrist Carl Jung discusses his parents. They were devoted and devout people (his father was a minister). Jung writes of his father: "He did a great deal of good. Far too much, and as a result was usually irritable. Both parents made great efforts to live devout lives with the result that there were angry scenes between them too frequently. These difficulties, understandably enough, later shattered my father's faith."[8] I suspect that most of us have had some experience with people carrying too heavy a burden of virtuousness.

An obsession with virtuousness also tends to produce the "reformer mentality." This belongs to the person who thinks himself (or herself) qualified to impose moral standards on others. If necessary, he will destroy other people in order to do that, so sure is he of his beliefs. A well-known example is the Christian reformer who, in the rage of his virtuousness, felt it was impossible to tolerate a pagan community. Political and social causes, too, have attracted reformers.

In addition, a strong sense of virtue reduces opportunities for spiritual growth. To grow in emotional maturity and understanding, we must have flexible standards. None of our beliefs can be sacrosanct. We must feel free to recognize our shortcomings, weaknesses, venality—we must feel vulnerable. Virtuous people cannot do this. Why should they? They are already "good."

To put this subject in a different light, let us consider some of the best-known virtues. All of us have used these cover-ups from time to time and sensed them in the behavior of other people.

Righteousness. Friedrich Nietzsche, the philosopher, used to refer to the "stinking shop in which we manufacture our spurious and pseudo ideals" and the "righteousness and innocence which destroy us without hope of salvation." Jesus spoke about the "hidden deceivers" and "wolves who appear clothed in the guise of lambs." Through the years, I have observed over and over that the person who is most deeply worried about his (or her) temptations to sin is the one who makes the strongest claim to righteousness. Trying to act as a model of decorum, propriety, and good intentions, he is destroyed inside by his righteousness while he strives to preserve the shell. "I will always do the right thing, whatever the consequences," he may say. Or, "I never act until I can tell right from wrong." By pretending to knowledge that is not really there, he complicates the task of those who are more honest and makes genuine achievement on their part more difficult than ever. Thus there is great wisdom in the psalmist's prayer: "Clear thou me from hidden faults. Keep back thy servant also from presumptuous sins." (Ps. 19:12–13.)

Love of justice. Everyone is in favor of justice; hence love of justice is an attractive virtue, because people find it hard to criticize the person proclaiming it. Almost all of us have felt at one time or another, though perhaps we could not put our finger on it, that a virtuous person's love of justice was not that desire at all; it was really hatred. Of course, we are talking about degrees of behavior now—about strong, consuming desires rather than ordinary wishes—but there is little doubt that cries for justice are often a cover-up for hatred and resentment.

Integrity. People who make a show of their high-level principles and complete devotion to ideals are suspect in most people's minds, and for good reason. Strongly professed integrity can be a nice way indeed of covering up inflexibility, brittleness, uncertainty. What the virtuous person forgets is that a healthy sense of uncertainty (that is, the uncertainty that an honest person feels in considering a situation, as distinct from the chronic uncertainty that masks insecurity) is a necessity for spiritual growth. If one or the other must be called a virtue, uncertainty would rank ahead of certainty.

Patience. During periods such as the mid-1960's, when civil rights disturbances preoccupied the nation, the virtue of patience may be extolled repeatedly. Patience is a fine quality and no thoughtful person questions its value. This may be why it is a popular cover-up when we seek to avoid the painful necessity of dealing with dangerous problems, such as, in the 1960's, when severe antiblack discrimination was still a reality. Unable to face up to the sins of society, our colleagues, a dominating employer, or some group moving in the wrong direction, we hide our cowardice under the virtue of patience.

Kindness and courtesy. These are important qualities for everyday living and I do not minimize them. Many of us have observed, though, that an outward expression of kindness or a show of courtesy may be a cover for indifference or antagonism. Where there is a creative relationship among two or more persons, there is less need for the so-called rules of courtesy because the individuals care for one another. They do not need to reassure one another by observing rules, because their mutual concern is understood.

Let me cite an example. You have a friend in trouble. His or her need is for more than kindness; the need is to see himself or herself from another's standpoint. For you, the most important thing is to be honest with that person. You have to open a window for your friend. This is hard to do—it may seem cruel and hurtful. And so you will be tempted to take the way out of kindness, of telling the person what he or she wants to hear, of exuding warmth and friendship. However, if you go this way, you do your friend no favor. Your kindness is but a frosting: *indifference* to your friend is what you are really exhibiting, or possibly even hate and resentment. Thus, kind and gentle behavior may be just another way of saying, "Who cares?"

Forgiveness. Sometimes when we hear a person say, "I forgive you," we wince. We cannot say why, but we know those are the wrong words. What we sense intuitively is the person's false pride of presuming to know how we should act; the forgiveness comes out of a sense of superiority! Whenever we find ourselves thinking, as Jesus is reputed to have said on the cross, "Forgive them, for they know not what they do," we need to question whether our lovely sense of forgiveness is a cover for arrogance. For possibly the attitude we are really taking is, "I know what they do, and I, knowing that, am above it and would not do it."

Devotion to hard work. Long working hours and devotion to a job is respected behavior in our society. Therefore it can be a convenient evasion. I would generalize that whenever we see a person who finds virtually nothing rewarding in life but work, that person is trying to avoid coming to terms with a weakness or sinful predilection. The weakness may be a sense of guilt about not really caring for members of the family. It may be a sense that life is meaningless, with work becoming a substitute for more intrinsic values that are not perceived. Righteous expressions about the importance of hard work may also mask feelings of materialism. In this case, acquiring wealth or fame is what we are really after, but since we feel uneasy about putting it in those terms, we use a well-known virtue for a disguise.

How do we deal with temptations like those described? The most important approach is willingness to accept the idea that "the devil is my brother." There is much evil in the world and it cannot be washed out of any of us. Admittedly, this is not a suitable philosophy for those who believe in the perfectibility of man or supernatural revelations.

By accepting the reality of evil I do not mean that we lie down in front of it. I do not espouse some ideal of passive resistance. If we are going to work for God in this world, we must fight for our ideals—but ideals based on recognition of our weaknesses, not the righteous ideals of the fanatic. In my view, the real idealist is the one who holds to his (or her) principles and dreams in spite of his deficiencies and the errors of friends. He fights his limitations every step of the way, not by hating them but by accepting them as part of himself. It is in this spirit that I propose to describe, in the next section, what seem to me to be the seven most destructive sins in contemporary society.

Robert Frost said he had a "lover's quarrel with the world." It is a statement worth meditating on. He loved the world but knew it had to be wrestled with. He knew himself on the same grounds. He loved his friends and his country but knew they were far from perfect. America was hard to see, he said in one poem; many people had testified to that fact. "They could not see it from outside—Or inside either for that matter."[9]

So we quarrel but we love. We fight but we accept. And I would hope that we criticize but not too harshly. Often, it seems to me, we expect too much of ourselves.

I hear people berating themselves because they have not recovered quickly enough from illnesses, yet they are improving steadily and might instead be taking great pride in their progress. I read sharp criticisms of my city's leadership, yet it is wrestling with extremely difficult conditions, and not giving up, and it could well be congratulated for what it is doing. I see spokesmen of different groups condemning the Federal Government and Americans in general, but it should be pointed out that this nation has come a very long way in two hundred years. It was not much more than a century ago that slavery was an organized, accepted institution here. Less than a century ago the governor of a Western state could publicly suggest the extermination of Indians.[10] Only a few decades ago practically everyone glorified war and the mass destruction of enemy cities.

Sometimes we talk of Christianity as if it had always been, yet its life on earth has been but a moment of man's time. A friend of mine runs a sizable company that celebrated the employees who had been on the payroll for thirty-five years or more. A large party for these persons was staged in a banquet room. I was one of the guests and I realized, as I met many of the thirty-five-year employees and looked around, that the years of service represented just in that room exceeded the time since the birth of Jesus!

Part II

SEVEN DEADLY
SINS OF TODAY

CHAPTER 4

Ignorance

"Where ignorance is bliss, 'Tis folly to be wise,"
Thomas Gray wrote. This proverbial saying may have
made sense at times in the past, and it may be valid in
trivial situations today. But ignorance is no longer bliss
in typical situations. In fact, ignorance is a great sin,
and ignorance of sin could be the worst sin of all. We
need to be more knowledgeable, more aware, better
informed. In the past, the price of ignorance was that
a person or a nation did not get ahead in the world.
Today the price has escalated, though lack of achievement is still part of it. Nowadays when we consider
ignorance we consider the question of our survival.

Let us examine four areas where ignorance is a
deadly sin in the sense described earlier; that is, it
interferes with the creative process of life. These areas
are not the only ones where ignorance is a sin. Many
readers will want to add to the list.

First, there is the nature of God. If God is defined as
the most important power in the world, we cannot
afford to be ignorant of him. How can we live success-

fully if we do not know about something on which we are dependent? Even if one decides that there is no God —that is, no creative force on which we are dependent —knowledge is crucial. For then the important thing becomes understanding the nature of our world and its principles of operation so that people can live more intelligently. In short, we must know what is good for humanity. It will no longer do to use the term "God" casually, whimsically, or sentimentally. And if we find we cannot learn about him, we should dismiss him and waste no more time on the question.

Are qualities such as gentleness, kindness, appreciation, love, self-sacrifice, and concern for growth the crucial ones for growth and creativity? If not, let us not bother with them. If they are, then we must know how and why they are good, for our future depends on developing them. How important is strength? What are the effects of qualities such as power, domination, race, and pride? We can never find out if we do not know what God is. If we know, we can begin to search out those qualities and processes which will help us express him. We can begin to cultivate those attitudes which will let him work through us. Seeking guidelines for living without factual knowledge of God that all can respect is like playing tennis without court lines; there is no way of telling what is in or out, good or bad.

Second is the area of human evolution. No longer can we afford to trust the evolutionary process; we must learn how to steer it. For millions of years evolution went on without active interference from any source. Mutations produced ever-new forms of life, including the higher forms we call man. Now man has become a partner in the evolutionary process. He is not just something to be moved around or abandoned when a better mutation comes along; he himself is an agent. He tinkers with the process, experiments with it, learns something about it, tinkers some more. Some experts believe that he is nearing the point where he can take over much of the process and direct it. In fact, some experts wonder if man will develop a new species. Do we continue as Homo sapiens related to this natural world of ours or do we create a new form unrelated to the natural world and not subject to the evolutionary process? It is a serious question.

Until the early part of the twentieth century, man's conscious objective was to reproduce as much as he could. Greater quantity of the species is still the biological goal of animal life. But quality, not quantity, must now be man's aim, as anyone who looks thoughtfully at population trends can see. Although a few societies and governments have worked hard to assure population control, the world's people in general have not yet accepted the need and so have not acted to meet it.

Either we learn how to improve the quality of life, the environment, and the people or we head toward destruction and let another species take over. Can there be any serious question about that? The role of physical fitness has changed too. Knowledge, understanding, and spirituality are far more important to survival now, with physical fitness being valuable mainly as an aid to health. Anthropology, biology, psychology, genetics, physics, chemistry, economics—all these areas of knowledge, and others as well, are essential if we are to direct the evolution of humanity wisely.

Much of the time, we act as if man were fated to live on earth forever, as if our destiny were settled. That is not true. Our genius, conscious awareness, is only an evolutionary experiment. We are a young form of life on this planet—many species that existed many times longer than we have were extinguished. It is not at all clear that the qualities of Homo sapiens have survival value. We are facing, I believe, an epochal crisis—not a crisis of this decade or this century but a crisis involving the entire future of man. Ignorance is not bliss in meeting this crisis.

Third, ignorance of ourselves and our relatedness is a sin. We have accepted myths about who the good and the bad people are. Almost always the fine, gentle, and loving people are the ones we haven't quarreled with lately, while the bad people are the ones who have given us trouble. These myths have no validity and must be rejected. We can no longer assume that in the noblest and most placid of us there are no fires burning, no aggressions, no desires for revenge. Our sociopolitical enemies do not monopolize such tendencies. What could be clearer to anyone who examines history, psychology, or comparative culture? Yet we talk and act repeatedly as if the opposite were true.

We must take the demonic into ourselves, examine our depravity, understand our weaknesses. Ignorance is not bliss in this task either. It can be demonstrated scientifically, I believe, that no one is free of the most destructive, antisocial tendencies. He or she may be a wonderful, creative person, but the malicious tendencies are still present. Failure to recognize them can be terribly destructive.

If understanding our relatedness is essential to our spiritual development, then we should apply ourselves to that subject with the same verve, energy, and intelligence that we have given to the building of roads, houses, factories, and products. Increased spiritual awareness would mean, for instance, that no businessman would pursue a course of action just for his firm or company. He or she would see business as of little importance compared to the overall welfare of the community. If businessmen gave anywhere near as much attention to relatedness as to internal functions such as finance, production, and salesmanship, community leaders all across the United States would not have to be fighting business because of pollution, would they? Management tends to defend pollution on the basis that countermeasures are too expensive. Not often, however, are the costs to the company and the labor force put in realistic perspective with the costs to the community. There is a good reason for this oversight. How many companies know very much about their relatedness to the community?

Fourth is the problem of how to build a great society. We do not yet know what the qualities and processes of a great society are—we only know that they will not just happen. After spending two hundred years and vast amounts of energy in the cultivation of a technological society and in the training of people to manage it and use it, we are now beginning to wonder if we can afford the machinery or our trained desires for its products. Survival values may indeed be stronger in a technologically underdeveloped country such as China.

We are not going to preserve and enhance our freedoms by counting on good intentions. Do we really know what freedom is? Are intelligent people agreed that freedom is protected by closing down certain movies, banning certain books, requiring certain kinds of clothes and hairdos at work? Or by maintaining various types of surveillance by law enforcement agencies? Or by storing enormous amounts of personal data about individuals on central electronic files available to municipal officials, credit companies, the police, and other groups?

Take economic policy as another case in point. We are supposed to be a great nation economically—the smartest there is. But do we have enough knowledge even in this area? Not long ago there was a food shortage, prices went up sharply, and so Washington instituted price controls. Then we saw photographs in the newspapers of farmers destroying hundreds of thousands of little chicks. The farmers said that because of price controls they could not afford to raise the chickens. What important pieces of knowledge were missing there? Or take economic forecasting. It was supposed to be a science—thousands of organizations were using it. But after the abysmal errors in the early 1970's and the fierce debates of experts over a series of basic assumptions used in forecasting, many people began to wonder whether any forecast could be believed again.

How much bliss is there in our ignorance of foreign aid? Agreeing that there are too many people in India, we help the Indian government to set up birth control programs. But at the same time our sense of humanity spurs us to send over medical and public health teams. Result: the population grows faster than ever. What knowledge is lacking here?

What about crime and punishment? Our prisons and criminal proceedings have appalled the experts for years. The system is stupid from a qualitative, psychological standpoint, and if there is any doubt about that, the statistics confirm that prisons do not save criminals but turn them into persons who are worse off by the time they are returned to society. But that does not stop us: we go on building more prisons and incarcerating more people. Again, ignorance is destroying a part of the social fabric.

We could cite many other examples, but the point should now be clear: The genius we have and must cultivate is conscious awareness. We must become more deeply, profoundly, and sensitively aware of who and what we are and of how all the parts are dynamically related in an indivisible organic whole. We must become increasingly aware of and responsive to emerging new relationships. We must become so good at this spiritually demanding task that we have little time, energy, or need for mere physical maintenance, the preservation of what has been, or winning victories over others. Jonas Salk, the scientist who pioneered in developing an antipolio vaccine, has concluded:

> Therefore it is necessary for man generally to acquire what some innately possess, i.e., wisdom to know the difference between the constructive and the uselessly destructive and to be able to act accordingly. We refer to awareness of the consequences of choices and of alternatives leading either to continued existence in the process of being and becoming or to destruction and nonexistence. . . .
>
> Eventually the struggle in the human domain will be between the wise and the nonwise.[11]

But why is ignorance a deadly sin? Why is it not simply a problem for educators and social scientists?

Ignorance is a deadly sin because it reduces our capacity for human fulfillment and for appreciation of the goodness of God. Ignorance is therefore a concern for religion, because religion must deal with whatever is important for human fulfillment. Thus, religion is concerned with the totality of life. There is nothing important to human life, for whatever reason, that is outside religion's scope of concern. It is particularly concerned with selecting, from all the phantasmagoria of experience, those qualities, attitudes, ideas, and realities which are most to be treasured because they are most important. It is clear, therefore, that critical, conscious awareness and judgment are of prime importance and that ignorance is a destructive impediment.

Of course, ignorance is the concern of educators, social scientists, and the media as well as of the church. In truth it must be the concern of everyone. Those specialists and nonspecialists who work to overcome ignorance, in whatever area, are performing a religious task. Religion in and of itself—that is, the institutional church—has neither the tools nor the personnel to eliminate ignorance. It is an absurd assumption, though one that is almost universally held, that religious activities are the exclusive concern of the church. The peculiar function of the church is to celebrate religious values, but these values do not reside *in* the church. They are created in the course of everyday human activity regardless of whether the activity is thought of as religious. Great growth in religion and therefore in the intelligent direction of our lives will take place when we realize more fully that all life is important and that any place or activity may be sacred. At such time, religion will be the universal concern of intelligent persons, for that will be the name they give to their search for a rich and abundant life.

Religion has not been noted for its rigorous application of brainpower. That is why it is failing. It is geared to the simple morality and homely community of times long since passed. A religion that is not only premodern, prescientific, and preindustrial but also pre-Renaissance and premedieval cannot guide us in a postmodern world. The whole nature of religion must be transformed or it will die.

How will it be transformed? Not by jazzing up the sacraments to make them more popular and appealing. Not by celebrating the Lord's Supper with guitars, voice choruses, and dancing troupes. Not by more decoration in church buildings. Those acts do not make the religious process more intelligible, they only make it more appealing. Efforts to increase appeal are fine and I like them, but how can so many religious leaders assume that such decorations can take the place of new understandings? We hear almost every week of new suggestions for regenerating religion, but when did a prominent official last speak of the necessity of transforming our religious beliefs? Not just tinkering with rules or procedures or language or forms, but radically revising basic tenets?

Never in the history of man has religion been so important as it is today, and never in modern history has it been so weak. Young people are leaving the church because it is not making sense to them intellectually. Traditional religion does not conform to the world as they and their teachers know it, does not reflect the truth as they see it, is not relevant to daily problems as they experience them. They will not go to the blind to be led, no matter how loudly we may bewail their lack of interest and concern.

What do we need to make our religion relevant and valid for people today—not just for older people and those who see poetic truths in the classic faiths but also for young people, scientists, professionals, skeptics, busy public officials? We need a new statement of the nature of man. We cannot go on assuming, as we have, that the universe has a purpose and that man is its predestined end and protected darling. We cannot go on assuming that man is a basically faulted creature but one that will be ultimately redeemed by divine power. We have the understanding and the techniques now to state more clearly and in more usable form the contradictory, polarized, ambivalent, confusing, and wonderful nature of man.

We need a new concept of sin, one that goes much deeper and farther than the Biblical story of disobedience or the traditional religious prohibitions and commandments. We need a concept of man that does not assume that his religious nature is a peculiar gift given to particular people at particular places and times. We need comforts and rewards that do not lie in a promised supernatural realm but that can be realized in the world we know. We need a new statement of values and their meaning—values that recognize man's nature as both animal and intellectual, that are not based on a primitively conceived hope that things are good in the beyond though all may be bad here, that build on experiential knowledge of man's limitations and aspirations.

We need a philosophy that does not count on supernatural intervention. Make no mistake, even those of us who pretend to be modern in our thinking harbor a lingering suspicion that somehow or other man is fated to come out all right, that his travails will be made up for, and that an individual's growth will continue after he or she dies. What must we learn to live in a world of a natural God who will not, like the traditional supernatural God, save us from ourselves? How are we to live in a world where hope for future redemption in another place, for increasing millions of the population, is totally unrealistic and unattractive?

The conflict between wisdom and ignorance is old. It seems astonishing that Christianity should have contributed to it, since the prophets in the Old Testament were aware that life was complicated and knew that the only way to survival was through wisdom. Somehow reverence for understanding was lost along the way. We must find that reverence again. In the words of Job:

> Man puts his hand to the flinty rock,
>   and overturns mountains by the roots.
> He cuts out channels in the rocks,
>   and his eye sees every precious thing.

He binds up the streams so they do not trickle,
and the thing that is hid he brings forth to light.
But where shall wisdom be found?
And where is the place of understanding?

. . . .
It cannot be gotten for gold,
and silver cannot be weighed as its price.
It cannot be valued in the gold of Ophir,
in precious onyx or sapphire.
Gold and glass cannot equal it,
nor can it be exchanged for jewels of fine gold.
No mention shall be made of coral or of crystal;
the price of wisdom is above pearls.
The topaz of Ethiopia cannot compare with it,
nor can it be valued in pure gold.

(Job 28:9–19)

CHAPTER 5

Arrogance

Arrogance is an attitude and a relationship. It might be characterized as a feeling of superiority, a disposition to shut out, a tendency to be dogmatic. When we are arrogant we feel and act as if we were not dependent on others; we display absolute conviction in our beliefs, groups, or institutions, as though they stood above and beyond others. The ultimate of arrogance is the shutting out of God; we assume self-containment and the ability to do it alone.

Although, as we shall see later, there has been much arrogance in Christianity, the Bible contains some eloquent warnings about this quality. For instance, in the Old Testament, Ezekiel is told to set his face against the king of Egypt and report that the Lord says:

> Behold, I am against you,
>   Pharaoh king of Egypt,
> the great dragon that lies
>   in the midst of his streams,
> that says, "My Nile is my own;

I made it."
I will put hooks in your jaws,
and make the fish of your streams
stick to your scales.
. . . .

Because you said, "The Nile is mine, and I made it,"
therefore, behold, I am against you, and against your
streams, and I will make the land of Egypt an utter waste
and desolation, from Migdol to Syene, as far as the border
of Ethiopia. (Ezek. 29:3–4, 9–10.)

Arrogance is the feeling that "this is my river—I
made it." This strength is my strength. This power
belongs to me and to no one else. Such an attitude is not
restricted to certain people; it is universal. There is no
time and place where it cannot be found. But perhaps
it is most conspicuous among people who are successful at the times of their greatest success. It should be
clear that arrogance does not necessarily show in one's
manner. It may be well masked by outward friendli-
ness, courtesy, and humor.

What causes arrogance? I suspect that ignorance
may be the ultimate explanation. In fact, ignorance of
one's ignorance is another way to define arrogance.
The attitude is caused also by fear, insecurity, and uncertainty—qualities that, paradoxically, are prominent at the peak of material success and prestige.
When we need to overcome a sense of futility, dependency, and anxiety we are likely to become arrogant.
Arrogance is a universal characteristic, because fear is
universal. There is no end of ways in which we can see
and hear arrogance every day.

In more conceptual terms, arrogance is the result of
what might be called semitranscendence. If we were
at the animal level, unknowing and unaware and dependent on the creative process without consciously
participating in it, we would not be arrogant. At the

other extreme, if we were Godlike, we would not be arrogant either. We would have no fear of being dragged down, no anxiety about situations, relationships, and dependencies—we would be above all that. The trouble is that we are right in between those two levels.

Feeling weak and unsure, we reach for certainty. Finding that we cannot achieve it, we pretend we have it. "We've got it made," we say. "We're above it now." A young woman made these observations in a letter to me:

> The sensation of isolation has us striving for securities, be they material, social, emotional, or religious, that become our rock island in a sea of the unknown, to which we cling desperately. We eagerly build more securities into our rock island, which isolates us even more from the sea of life, and then we feel even more alienated and separated and so even more insecure and frightened.

This is a simple, beautiful description of the human process that creates arrogance. We seek it most when we should have it least. Intellectual pride is a form of arrogance. We presume that we are above this group or that need because of our knowledge, but, knowing that knowledge changes, we have to establish a pretense that ours is absolute truth. Nothing must shake our rock island. Preoccupation with power is a form of arrogance. It is not enough for us to have a threefold or fourfold overkill power against the Russians (or for them to have it against us). We must have more! In our semi-transcendence we want to be transcendent, above the threat, like God. Spiritual pride is a form of arrogance, too. We feel weak and fearful in the midst of all this worldly uncertainty. We want to come through as perfect, so we devise and claim to possess a sure formula for salvation.

Does arrogance work for us? Yes and no. If I am frightened but do not show it, if I am unsure but do not let anyone see it, I may achieve something more easily and quickly. Our society looks to the strong and completely confident person to compensate for its own fears and weaknesses and gives that person many of the prizes. As a short-run success formula, arrogance often works.

So we train our children to try always to be right. As parents, we feel a compulsion to set ourselves up in front of them as adults who are always right. As leaders we seek to show no signs of weakness to our followers. When we make a decision it must be as though there were no other right decision. A military commander must look absolutely confident in front of his men, or they may desert him. Nor do most politicians feel that they can afford to indicate any uncertainty. Some who did, like Adlai Stevenson in the 1950's, paid for their point of view in votes. As a minister I know all too well the value of an outward appearance of absolute confidence and rightness. Many audiences for clergymen tend to react with the attitude, "If he doesn't *know*, why listen to him?" At funerals where I express wonder and uncertainty about the meaning of death, I may find listeners sinking away from me. But I know that if I can tell them I have a clear, decisive explanation, I can carry them along with me.

All great evangelists have been supremely confident; nearly all great military leaders have been. Leaders of totalitarian regimes have to be; if Hitler had ever indicated doubts about German supremacy or racial genocide, he would have lost his hold on his followers. Unswerving, unquestioning confidence is a key element of good gamesmanship too. I have experimented with it in card games and in athletics and I invite the reader to experiment with it. It can be effective.

When it works, we begin building a following of believers, helpers, and subordinates. Now when we feel a little unsure of ourselves we can look for confirmation to the people around us who bow and scrape or say "Yes, sir!" (if they do not run off and hide from our arrogance). This is one reason "good people" are likely to be arrogant. Years ago I read a report on the execution for murder of a woman in California. Near the end of her days when she was talking about her case without rancor she said, "The trouble with the good people is that they are always so sure they're right." Strong people on the side of justice, reform, or discipline of some sort are almost always noted for being "sure they're right."

But arrogance does not work *really*. That is, it does not save the individual from the needs that make him or her arrogant in the first place. Nor does it work from the standpoint of creative growth for a family, organization, or society. Let me explain why.

First, arrogance cannot work for the simple, fundamental reason that no one is above it all. We do *not* have it made. We are dependent on other people in countless ways. There is nothing we can do that is completely good. There is no virtue without vice. These qualities were discussed earlier.

Second, the psychology of arrogance works against us. The more we lay claim to the security of our rock island, the more insecure we become, because we know in our heart that security is an illusion. The tragic insecurity of the arrogant "strong man"—the hoarder, the patriarch, the empire builder, or the owner of a winning streak—is legend.

Third, and most significant, arrogance is basically and pervasively sinful. The more it shuts us off from feelings of dependence on others and the more it isolates us, the more it confines us to our own limited resources. There is no growth for us unless the sea comes in, unless there is some kind of infusion into our rock castle. Arrogance is destructive for the same reason that incest is. We must be challenged. We must feel prodded in order to change our ideas. We must get new blood. We must hear, see, and feel attitudes that may at first seem unwelcome. This is the story of creative growth in every form of life, human and nonhuman. The sin of arrogance may be small, and it often is; but if we put ourselves in a position for long where we cannot share with others, be intruded on, or get hurt by contrary ideas, we will stop changing. This is another way of saying that we will shut out the goodness of God, for God, as we have defined him, is evolution—opening up, breaking out, achieving greater awareness and understanding. The basic trouble with the "good people" is that they stop changing.

History and the contemporary scene are full of examples of the sinfulness of arrogance. I shall mention but ten instances here:

1. *Christianity's rejection of other religions.* In the organized Christian churches there has been a long history of rejecting other religious philosophies, moralities, and ways of life. Too often Christian leaders have assumed that they had it made. They were the chosen people of God, they had the absolute truth, their code was God's code, their understanding of salvation was absolutely correct. Therefore they could justify heaping horrors, cruelties, and injustices upon millions of people—North American Indians, Moslems, Arabs, Jews, dissenters, heretics of many types. If righteous and militant Christians had had the humility not to try to take the place of God and impose their ways on others, we would be much farther along the road to solving many of the problems that beset us in world society.

2. *Christianity's rejection of secularism and science.* In centuries past, officials of Christian churches were notorious for rejecting men such as Galileo, Copernicus, Harvey, the evolutionists, and numerous others. In many churches, Christians continue to fight secular understanding of life and the universe. This wasteful effort to become or pretend to be nondependent and nonrelated to wisdom from other sources is sinful not only because it has made Christianity destructive as an institution (e.g., its efforts to block scientists) but also because it has suppressed spiritual growth in the rank and file. Now Christianity is paying the price for its arrogance as church members defect from "dead" faiths.

It might be added that we are now seeing this situation turned around: secularists and scientists committing the same kind of sin that Christians committed. In pride over their computers, measurements, test tubes, spaceships, and other achievements, they are forgetting that there is something called the spirit which is qualitative, not quantitative, and extremely important to mankind.

3. *Whites' rejection of nonwhites.* How many remarkable black human beings have died in the United States without ever having had a chance to apply their wonderful talents? How many Chinese, Japanese, Mexicans, and brown-skinned people? We have shut them out, dominated them, refused to allow them to grow and participate. This was a colossal sin. How much genius has this country lost as a result of white supremacy?

4. *National supremacy.* A substantial part of the U.S. electorate still considers this country a kind of knight in white armor opposed to the Soviet Union as the black knight. We are good, they are evil. Even today we find some Americans feeling that they must ex-

plain themselves if they say something good about the Russians. Perhaps we could afford this attitude in the eighteenth and nineteenth centuries, but it amounts to a grievous and costly sin today. Our arrogance toward other nations—countries in Southeast Asia and South America, for example—has also diminished us.

5. *Aristocratic superiority.* Despite our democratic ideals, we still have strong tendencies toward upper-level group control and domination. Millions of poor, ignorant, untutored people have had little opportunity to contribute their genius. In Abraham Lincoln we have one of the world's finest symbols of what can come from a simple peasant type. But how many millions of potential Abraham Lincolns never had a chance?

6. *Intellectual aloofness.* I mention this sin because, it seems to me, we are in danger of developing a new aristocracy of intellectuals. This movement is an expression of a desire for isolation, nondependency, and "staying above it all." In a more subtle way it is as sinful as are other forms of arrogance. Where is there more snobbery in our country than on college and university campuses? The backlash can be strong. When there are revolutions, as in Russia in 1917 and in Germany in the 1930's, the first people the revolutionaries may go after are the professors. The professors are vulnerable because they have separated and isolated themselves.

7. *Male chauvinism.* Only in this century did women get the vote, and not until the late 1960's did an earnest movement for equal job opportunity for the sexes begin. We can never know what American civilization has lost because of male arrogance. Of course, the battle is far from won. We do not even have a language yet that is nondiscriminatory. Is it not absurd to refer to a person as "he," "him," or "himself"? (We can always

say "he or she," "him or her," and so on, but that is cumbersome.) We lack pronouns for the individual as a human being regardless of sex.

8. *Patronizing of children.* We care for our children, love them, and educate them. But we feel that we are superior and so we never see and hear qualities of beauty, wonder, and imagination that come from children. In this scientific, mechanical, intellectual world of ours, the sin of adult superiority may be more damaging than it ever was.

9. *Political elitism.* The arrogance of many of the White House Staff in the early 1970's was frightening and shocking. They made themselves superior to their party, nondependent on Congress, above the Constitution; in overreaching themselves they destroyed themselves. Emperors and kings have done the same thing —Napoleon, Alexander, Genghis Khan, Nicholas II, George III, Hirohito. Sophocles, Aeschylus, and other Greek dramatists wrote about the sin of arrogant leadership—it was the point of *Oedipus* and *Prometheus,* for instance. Shakespeare dramatized that sin in *Macbeth* and *King Lear.* "The Nile is mine, and I made it"—the Pharaoh's words continue to echo in political councils.

10. *Disdain of nature.* Soon we will not need the animals anymore, some authorities are saying. We will not need the rain, the changes of weather, the cold. We will make our own world, create our own environment. We will build cities under the sea and put domes over our land. We are not dependent on nature anymore. Such stupidity and arrogance! Indeed, the shutting out of nature may well be the *final* sin, because it is such a caustic, assertive expression of superiority.

Putting Down Arrogance

Tendencies toward arrogance are in all of us. How are we to cope with them? Learning to accept our dependency is perhaps the most important step, recognizing that we cannot save ourselves apart from the rest of humanity and nature. Coming to terms with this fact is the best counter to fear and anxiety. The Nile is not ours, it is God's. Our power and glory is God working through us. We are a part of the whole, not a separate part—this is the essence of humility.

This general truth is so apparent that we may not think about it. Let me set forth a rationale for it—five simple propositions that justify humility:

1. *All life is insecure.* This goes for the most primitive forms right on up to the most complicated forms. No matter how confidently we approach the future, there is never a time when it is secure—for us, for the nation, or for the human race.

2. *All truths are partial.* There is no absolute truth that we know of. Some truths are more valuable, stable, and enduring than others, but the most basic and fundamental laws are subject to correction. The reassuring maxims that we often cite do not even have short-run value. It is said, "A good tree cannot bring forth bad fruit." Nonsense—it often does. What about, "A bad tree cannot bring good fruit"? That is equally unreliable, as every geneticist and historian knows. It is often stated, "A man cannot serve two masters." Yet there is no person today who can be a responsible, participating citizen without serving more than two masters, accepting them despite their conflicts and inconsistencies. Even inside a single corporation a person may be expected to serve two masters well, as ex-

perience at Dow Corning and other so-called matrix organizations teaches us.

A statement that has become almost sacred is, "You cannot serve both God and mammon." Proclamations to the contrary, the church owes its very existence to having served mammon to some degree. It seems clear to me that spiritual development itself must give some service to mammon. In a world where life depends on so many transactions, can God and mammon be separated? "He that is not for me is against me." This is nonsense too. Moreover, a person who is against me may on important occasions be for me. I may be for you as a friend and against the kind of activity in the community that you find interesting. I may be for you as a professional person—for instance, a surgeon or a lawyer—and against you as a personality.

3. *All viewpoints are limited.* No matter how important our viewpoints toward marriage, work, self-responsibility, child-rearing, taxation, and so on may seem to be, no matter how clear, no matter how valuable they have proven to be in our lives, they are limited and prejudiced. Though we may decide and act boldly, it should always be with the realization that we can see but a part of the picture.

4. *All solutions are limited, partial, and temporal.* If the first three propositions are valid, then so must this one be. There is no complete solution for war and peace, for the energy crisis, for dishonesty in government, or for disrespectful children.

5. *A compulsiveness to be right is neurotic.* Whenever our compulsions to do the right thing or the best thing are so strong that we feel unable to consider doing the opposite, we are in trouble. A compulsion to be right is almost invariably a sign of lack of real confidence in oneself, of unwillingness to face human nature as it is. There is enormous value in recognizing

that our strongest beliefs may be wrong. This recognition has been part of the genius of some of our greatest statesmen, and scientists point out that they sometimes make as much progress from wrong hypotheses as from right ones.

Henry Clay is given credit for the apparently virtuous statement, "I would rather be right than president." Could a person make a more arrogant statement than that? Either Clay was belittling the highest position in the land or he sought to ascribe to himself a superior virtue. Once and for all, he was right, others were wrong! Freely translated, the statement becomes: "I would rather be right than sensitive and aware. I would rather be right than noble. I would rather be right than humble, gentle, and understanding. I would rather be right than face the possibility of growth."

Henry Clay's example is not unknown to us parents. Would we rather be right than have the love of our children? Many of us act as though we would. Would we rather be right than have our children independent and adventurous? Many of us act as though we would. Our children would come to have more genuine affection for us, I suspect, if they realized that we could be wrong as well as right. They would become better able to distinguish right from wrong if they had to discover it for themselves rather than lean on their parents for the knowledge.

I am not arguing for sloppy standards of behavior or wishy-washy attitudes and convictions. I am arguing that we should be humble enough not to try to take on ourselves the role of God. The conclusion that seems most clearly "right" to us is still human and fallible. To put it in more classical terms, the time when God seems to speak loudest to us is when we should wonder if it is really the voice of God.

To the degree that we do not accept these five rules, we are in danger of acting arrogantly. We make ourselves prone to intolerance and willing to inflict physical torture on our neighbors as the Christian church did in the Middle Ages and as Stalin did in the Soviet Union. The Watergate break-in and cover-up, the ruthless law-and-order policy of the 1968 Presidential Convention in Chicago, efforts to restrict free speech, invasions of privacy—these less violent acts, too, can be justified if exceptions to the rules are made.

We are going to have to learn to live with choices in the gray. For example, we cannot find choices of leadership at the community or national levels that are clear choices between right and wrong. There will be qualities in each of the opposing candidates that we regard as strong and positive, other tendencies that we find dangerous. We can campaign vigorously for one or the other and make our choices joyously, but we must do so knowing that we can see only partial truths. This is another way of saying that we must be prepared constantly for change. This attitude is the mark of a mature and religious people.

CHAPTER 6

Greed

One of Leo Tolstoy's stories deals with a peasant who is a successful small farmer. The peasant works his land well and diligently, but his holdings are small and he complains that he does not have more land. He envies the prominent landowners for their large acreages. One day the peasant's complaints come to the attention of the local ruler, who makes a special offer. In view of the fact that the peasant is a good citizen and has worked his holdings hard and well, the ruler will give him all the land he can circle between sunrise and midday. But the ruler stipulates that the peasant must be back precisely where he started at twelve noon or before. If he does not get back to the starting point, he does not get the land.

On the appointed day the peasant's friends and neighbors gather to watch. Promptly at sunrise he starts out. Although some of the onlookers leave for a while to go about their business, everyone is back by midmorning to wait for their friend to return. At ten thirty he is not in sight. At eleven there is still no sign of him. When there is no sign of him at eleven fifteen, they begin to worry. Finally at eleven thirty they see him in the distance and realize that it is going to be nip and tuck whether he can make it to the starting point in time. Some friends run out to greet and encourage him. The peasant runs, stumbles and falls, gets up and walks, tries to run again, stumbles once more—while the clock continues mercilessly on its way. But sure enough, the peasant does just make it in time. With one minute to spare, he staggers across the finish line. All the land is his! Then he falls dead.

The story is simple and mythlike; there are many similar tales. They may remind us of the tale of the dog with a bone in his mouth who sees in the reflection of the water what looks like another bone, grabs for it, and loses the one he has.

Arnold Toynbee has characterized our times as the Age of Greed. That may be, but greed is not a passing characteristic. It is a universal trait. Bertrand Russell has stated that greed is simply another name for life itself: to live *is* to desire and seek to possess. Greed has characterized all ages in the history of man—this is why I call it a basic sin. We cannot exorcise it in some way. Our desire to hold and accumulate is necessary for civilization to progress. But strangely enough, greed is not one of the classical seven deadly sins (see Chapter 1). It *is* a part of envy, avarice, gluttony, and lust, yet it is stronger, broader, and more destructive than are those deadly sins of old.

Like arrogance, greed is caused by fear and insecurity. We are not sure that the world will provide, or, to use religious terminology, not sure that the Lord will provide. Worrying that we will not be able to meet our needs tomorrow, we reach for more than we need now. "Get it while the getting is good." Thus, greed is a function of our capacity to think, see ahead, and plan.

A person's greed is more potent and overreaching than an animal's—there is practically no limit to the bounds of greed in man. On the other hand, human nature has a capacity to contain and limit greed that animal nature does not. To the extent that we can gain confidence in the capacity of our fellowman to share and in the capacity of ourselves to live at peace in the world, we are not greedy. One of Jesus' most beautiful insights is:

> Ask, and it will be given you; seek, and you will find; knock, and it will be opened to you. For every one who asks receives, and he who seeks finds, and to him who knocks it will be opened. What father among you, if his son asks for a fish, will instead of a fish give him a serpent; or if he asks for an egg, will give him a scorpion? (Luke 11:9–12.)

But greed also comes from feelings of emptiness, futility, triviality. We make ends out of means because the means are not enough to feed on. However, when we try to make an end out of a means such as food and drink or power, we do not find the reward we set out to get. We are left hungry. I believe that this is what Toynbee and other philosophers have been telling us. We are feeding today on things that do not nourish us, madly pursuing purposes that do not satisfy. They will never satisfy us, no matter how much we gorge ourselves on them, because what we need is something else. Indeed, all great spiritual leaders have seen this truth. And all readers of this book are old enough to have experienced it, for it is writ large on the walls of our life.

Gluttony is one of the best everyday illustrations of greed. Gluttons eat and drink compulsively, but are they ever satisfied? The need for food is not the real need; there has been a neurotic transposition of the problem. In reality, gluttons are trying to satisfy an insecurity or fear by eating and drinking—and, of course, it doesn't work. They are like people driven by neurotic compulsions to keep washing their hands; the more they wash, the more they worry about not being clean. All the waters in the world cannot wash them clean enough. Echoes of Macbeth!

Why is greed a deadly sin instead of a lesser, or venial, sin? While gluttony and lust lead to health problems, family conflicts, and social disturbances, greed can do all that and much more. Wanting satisfactions that elude us, knowing not how to procure them, feeling increasingly worthless, frustrated, and angry, we turn on others—as well as on ourselves—with terrible vindictiveness. We strike out anywhere—it doesn't matter. The most convenient person or institution may be the object of our wrath.

Let us look at some illustrations. In each case, bear in mind that the object or activity described may be valid and necessary as a *means.* This is true, for example, of armed power and of money; the former is necessary for a nation that desires to stay independent, and the latter is necessary for a person who wishes to live above the public welfare level. What we shall consider is the function of such means when they are turned into goals.

Armed power. Competent men and women reach for power first in the effort to survive. Thus power is a legitimate need at the outset. But then the appetite seems to feed on itself and more and more power is sought. This was the story of kings, queens, barons, and the nobility in ancient times and the Middle Ages; it is the story of the nuclear and other arms races today. The U.S. Government finds that it is not enough to be equal to the Soviets in military might; we must be much more powerful than they. It was not enough for the U.S.S.R. to aggrandize its power by taking over part of Poland and several Baltic countries after World War II; it had to absorb Czechoslovakia and Hungary as well. We are like the archangel in Milton's *Paradise Lost*. It was not enough for him to be next to God! He had to become God. There is, it seems, no limit to our greed even in the realm of the spirit—even around "the throne of God."

Greed for armed power is a deadly sin because it could lead someday soon to the destruction of the human race. In the meantime it drains precious resources needed to make civilization healthier, more creative, and harmonious.

Applause and recognition. Almost everyone has seen this form of greed at work. It shows up in the famous actor or actress who, having retired earlier after many years of applause and recognition, finds that the old successes are not enough and so decides to make a comeback. It shows up in the middle-aged sex symbol who has to keep in the limelight; although fifty or sixty years old, he or she has to keep going—has not had enough. It shows up in the aging congressman or senator who, despite many years of wielding control over legislation, must keep maneuvering in order to stay in power.

As a minister and counselor, I find myself called on repeatedly to reassure people that they are worthy. They come begging for more praise. If they get it from me, they run to someone else who will reassure them yet again. They are never satisfied with what they hear. It is a disturbing experience to watch their futility and to try to meet their neurotic need.

Jealousy. Jealous people never have enough personal attention from spouses, children, parents, and friends. They want more and more love and support; no one living with them can satisfy them. Nothing short of total attention will do, and even this will not suffice. Lacking real love in their lives, they have to compensate by acquiring worshipers—but never get enough of them.

In *Othello,* Shakespeare has Iago say:

> O, beware, my lord, of jealousy;
> It is the green-ey'd monster which doth mock
> The meat it feeds on.

In the jealous person the green-eyed monster mocks the attention it feeds on; it cannot bear someone else's success in commanding attention. A friend of mine once told me how jealousy had influenced him. "A year ago I was promoted," he said. "It was a good promotion with increased reputation for me, a nice position in the company, much more money. I was so delighted I could hardly stand it. Yet inside of six weeks I was comparing myself with others and wondering why the company didn't pay me as much as it paid them. I believed I was a much better man than the company thought. I was worthy of more than I was getting." Is there anyone who has not had a similar experience in some form or other? The green-eyed monster lurks in the caverns of every human spirit. I know a few people who seldom experience the monster, but I do not know anyone who never experiences it.

This form of greed is deadly because it poisons our days. Resenting someone else's success, even a friend's, we find it hard to smile and offer congratulations. Why her? we ask ourselves. Why not me? Such misery we bring on ourselves! Is there not enough already without adding more? Here is what Aleksandr Solzhenitsyn writes:

It is enough if you don't freeze in the cold and if thirst and hunger don't claw at your insides. If your back isn't broken, if your feet can walk, if both arms can bend, if both eyes see, and if both ears hear, then whom should you envy? And why? Our envy of others devours us most of all.[12]

Life. The lust for immortality is an expression of greed. Of course, we won't say out loud that we want immortality, but in effect that is what we are saying when, after long and busy lives, we fight death. But if we could somehow be granted another fifty years, would we not again fight the thought of dying when that term is up?

In my experience, those who have lived rich, full lives and have found fulfillment are not so afraid to die when the time comes. It is those who have found life empty and meaningless who fight death. They are not satisfied with having shared for a time in the joys that people treasure—they want more for themselves. *Some* greed of this kind is found in all of us, because all of our lives seem lacking in some respects and society has helped none of us find fulfillment as well as it might have. Perhaps this is inevitable. But we need not come to the end desiring desperately for a little more. Quantity of life does not satisfy.

Money and possessions. One of the most conspicuous forms of greed in an acquisitive society is the lusting for ever more wealth and acquisitions. One of the rarest sights in this country is a person who lacks possessions yet feels proud of his life, or who, though never having made out in the commercial world, walks with dignity and self-appreciation. Far more common is the seventy-year-old business person who is still trying to make more money after a lifetime of earning—still trying to make a buck in some new way, or add to his or her estate, or finance a bigger house or car. We rarely question such a life-style. Instead, our society encourages it. How absurd! Surely a seventy-year-old person should not be on the same level of acquisition as a thirty-year-old is. Is there not more to life than going from youth to old age in an unending desire to accumulate possessions?

A society that values such an approach has no justification for survival, and I do not believe it can survive. Unless its eyes, mind, and heart are on the living of life, it will pass into evolutionary history, giving way to a society with different qualities. Therefore I see nothing admirable about a family moving from one place to another, taking itself away from one group of friends after another, pulling the children out of one school after another, all for the sake of gaining jobs with a little more money and getting ahead a little faster. I see nothing admirable about generals and admirals who, after being well rewarded during their military careers, turn to prestigious positions on corporate boards after retirement from the service, there to sell their reputations, contacts, and know-how in Washington circles. As President Harry Truman once said, surely a general can be expected to live with more dignity than that after retirement. Nor do I see anything admirable in a former president's taking a large tax deduction for the gift of his papers to the country. Despite having become wealthy and famous, Lyndon B. Johnson felt that he needed to achieve a financial gain from giving papers to a library raised in his honor. The fact that he was a dedicated public servant is beside the point. He never stopped taking all he could get. With our leaders setting examples like these, it is no wonder that at lesser levels there has been so much compulsive hoarding during times of shortage and war profiteering during times of national emergency.

These simple illustrations show how dangerous and unworkable greed is today. It may have been all right at one time in our history when there were not so many of us, when there was more space, and when we needed to accumulate for capital expansion. But it is not all right anymore. We are too crowded, too dependent on one another, and lacking in resources. As a nation, we can no longer afford greed. It is even less acceptable in international society. The greed of the "have" nations is becoming intolerable to the "have not" nations. The "haves" must learn to share or face the wrath of the many deprived millions. The means of retaliation are fast becoming available. Dr. Edward Teller, who helped develop the atomic and hydrogen bombs, has testified that between one hundred thousand and one million people now have the basic information to assemble nuclear weapons. This number is growing. Think what that could mean to a bitter, militant country that feels it has nothing to lose.

In short, we have come to the point where sharing, not aggrandizing, is the key to survival. We share or we die. Not the individual but the community, not competition but cooperation, not grabbing but helping— these are the keys to growth and creativity. I do not mean that the individual is no longer important or that power and accumulation are unnecessary. Personal brilliance and organizational pioneering will continue to be important. But individuals and groups must work more through the shared and sharing community. I see the word "greed" becoming a term for death, and sharing a term for life.

Ways of Coping

How are we to cope with our tendencies toward greed, jealousy, and gluttony? Let me suggest some ways.

First, part of the solution lies, as always, in the problem. If greed is created by our intelligence, then bad thinking and bad information are what we must deal with. The cure is not less intelligence but more. We must see more clearly that none of us can have everything. There are some things you can have that I cannot, and vice versa. This seems obvious enough when stated so bluntly, but it is a truth that eludes greedy people. They want all that you have plus what they already have.

Such greed is due in part, I am convinced, to our democratic, egalitarian philosophy. Inculcated in us is the belief that all people are created equal, meaning in this case that they start equal. Such nonsense! People do not start equal, nor do they stay equal; they have varying strengths and weaknesses. We do not all have equally loving, kind, and generous parents; we do not have equally good education; we are not exposed equally to inspiring and helpful people; we do not have equally stable emotions and constitutions. Yet, because of the egalitarian myth, we are not willing to let someone else have more, because that would indicate he or she is better than we are. The "keeping up with the Joneses" trait in our culture is a direct result. Seeing someone with more money, achievements, possessions, or friends than we have makes us resentful. We are led to feel that the inequality diminishes us. We must learn to accept ourselves for what we are with our varying needs, skills, capacities, and achievements.

Second, we can draw on experience to counteract greed and jealousy. Experience teaches us that we should not want everything, because everything has its costs. There is a cost to having children, a cost to being a public personality, a cost to being wealthy, a cost to being a fine athlete, a cost to being handsome or beautiful. Each one of these advantages is paid for, and although one by one the costs may seem worthwhile, the cumulative price is beyond the powers of any one person to pay. I suspect this is why Aeschylus suggested long ago that we have enough burdens to carry without adding that of jealousy:

> For few they are who have such inborn grace
> As to look up with love, and envy not
> When stands another on the height of weal.
> Deep in his heart, whom jealousy hath seized
> Her poison lurking doth enhance his load;
> For now beneath his proper woes he chafes,
> And sighs withal to see another's weal.[13]

So if I am a poor person looking with envy at a rich person, I should ask if I can afford the price of becoming rich. If I take the trouble to look into the personal experience of wealthy people, I might find that the price would cripple me. I may still want to pay it, but if I go through this exercise for several things I desire greedily, I will realize that not only is it impossible for me to have everything but that I do not really want everything.

Third, we can take satisfaction in the fact that, although we cannot have everything, some things are peculiarly ours. I find it wonderful to see the unique qualities that belong to people—qualities they own as no one else does. A special kindness characterizes this person, a certain understanding belongs to that person, an unusual ability is possessed by still another. Such qualities, when I discover them, strike me as becoming, befitting, and enhancing—the infinite shines through them as though they had been created that way by God from the beginning. To know what it is that belongs especially to us, in different combinations in each person, is a form of wisdom. It will save us from the misery of all those who are driven by ridiculous competition to seek things they would not want if they thought more wisely. One of the functions of religion should be to help us to gain this wisdom.

Fourth, love helps to overcome greed. The two qualities are totally incompatible. To the degree that we are envious or jealous, we are not loving, and to the degree that we are loving, we cannot be greedy. When we love, we are pleased when our friends have what they want. Love does not envy, love is not jealous, love is not glad when others go wrong, love is not resentful of the things other people enjoy and delight in—Paul saw such qualities in love when he wrote his beautiful first letter to the Corinthians.

I do not suggest complete self-denial, for there are legitimate forms of selfishness. For example, we must protect ourselves against the selfish demands of others. If we are weak and unsure, someone may move in and take us over for his or her own enhancement and selfish interests, perhaps under the camouflage of unselfish devotion. For the sake of the other as well as of ourselves we must guard against being used or we will lose our selves. There has never been a saint, including Jesus, who did not need to protect himself against the intrusions of others. We have obligations to become as complete a personality as possible, for our value to others depends on the quality of our own selves, and if we have no respect for ourselves, we can scarcely be of much value to another person. Joshua Liebman once quoted the reply of a psychiatrist to a woman who wanted to help others because she felt so mean and miserable herself: "Dear Madam, your truly magnificent shortcomings at present are too great. Nothing could prevent you from visiting them on victims of your humility. I advise that you love yourself more before you squander any love on others."[14]

Finally there is the question of how to muster the strength and understanding necessary to take the steps described. Can we do that if we are limited, as all of us are, in wisdom, experience, and capacity to love? There is one good answer: *discipline.* One time, after a discussion of how to deal with sin, a friend of mine remarked, "Yes, but that's easier said than done." I answered: "Of course it is. What else? How could anything be as easily done as said?" I know of no spiritual achievement that involves no effort. All our days we must work at it.

We do not easily lose resentment, or jealousy, or desires to keep up with the Joneses. We have to talk to ourselves to understand, and when our understanding starts to waiver, we must work on it again. When we see our love dissipating in jealousy, we must go back and question ourselves. "Who am I that I should have everything? Who am I that I must possess what I do and also have what another has? Besides, is that quality or possession really needed to keep me happy?" The ties of love do not grow automatically. They have to be strengthened, refreshed, renewed, and reexamined— and this requires discipline.

CHAPTER 7

Violence

A friend of mine made an observation that startled me. He said, "You know, it's probably the fate of 90 percent of all living creatures to be eaten alive." Now possibly it is not their fate to be eaten alive, but certainly it is their fate to be killed. For a long time we humans have been escaping the fate of being eaten; instead, we do the eating. This is one of the reasons that our population has grown so enormously, almost to the point where it is too large a burden on the resources of the world. Alfred Tennyson's famous phrase, "Nature, red in tooth and claw," applies to us, much as we hate to talk about it. The only life that maintains itself is that which is successful and is efficient in destroying and eating others. We hardly ever talk about or visit slaughterhouses, but they are central to our existence. We cover up our depradations as we do the ravages of death, so that we are not reminded of who we are and how we live.

The trouble is that man is more violent than animals precisely because he is human and has a mind that plans, directs, controls, and imagines. He will kill not only for the sake of food and clothing but also for the sheer pleasure of it. His imagination outruns his animal nature—he can conceive of all manner of ways of getting fun from the destruction of other life. For man, killing can be an artistic expression. He transforms need into art or recreation and pursues it beyond any genuine human necessity or value.

Violence has been defined as the capacity to make a corpse out of a human being or any living creature. That definition covers much of the discussion to follow, but it is helpful to use a more comprehensive definition. Let us think of violence as the use of coercion or compulsion to effect changes in another person or group without its free, voluntary consent and acquiescence. Violence almost always implies an invasion of a person from someone or some force outside. The person's integrity, dignity, selfhood, freedom, and rationality are violated. He (or she) is no longer making and choosing his own destiny.

The taking of a castle makes a good illustration to start with. There are two major ways to take a castle. It can be bombarded, stormed, breached, invaded, and overcome; or its occupants can be compelled to surrender by laying siege. The victims die by the sword in the first case; they surrender or succumb from thirst, starvation, and disease in the second. The end is basically the same in both instances.

Similarly, violence occurs in our daily lives when we are blackmailed, robbed, assaulted, or shot. It occurs also when we are forced to submit to another's demands as a result of pressure—when we are besieged until we give in. For instance, a student sit-in at a college administration building is a form of violence. What the demonstrators are doing is not different in principle from the action of an army that lays siege to

the castle (assuming the demonstrators are well organized and determined not to budge until the administration capitulates). The university officials do not die
of hunger or thirst, or have to surrender their positions, but they feel compelled to grant the demands of
the demonstrators. Their freedom to choose and their
integrity of choice are violated.

What about the boycott of a store? The object is to
"starve" the owner into meeting the demands of his
critics. The boycotters do not try to persuade with facts
and logical exposition of claims for justice. They seek
to impose their views and to compel particular actions.
A boycott, however passive, is a form of violence.

Massive demonstrations? Their aim is to coerce law-
makers to come to terms with the interests of the
demonstrators. The demand is made that "you accede
to our wishes or we will badger you until you do"—
again the same thing in principle as the siege of the
castle.

Violence takes more subtle forms. For instance, subliminal advertising on a movie or television screen
qualifies as a form of violence because the viewer is
not being allowed to make a conscious free choice.
Although no physical force is used, there is compulsion. Therefore we prohibit subliminal advertising by
law. Hypnosis is in a similar category, for the subject
is made to perform actions without really choosing.

Long before man's power and imagination became
great enough to threaten the existence of other species
—or his own—it was apparent that restraints needed to
be placed on violence. Moral codes are such restraints.
The earliest known rules in our culture were those of
Hammurabi of the Babylonian Empire. His codes, the
rules of the Jews contained in the Ten Commandments, and all other such precepts were basically the
same (Ex., ch. 20; Deut., ch. 5). They said in effect: "If

we are going to live together, if we are going to make it, we cannot intrude violently on one another. We must not kill one another. We must not steal from one another. We must not take another man's wife or another woman's husband, and we must not even lie about one another, for such lies can also lead to violence."

Today the ancient rules about violence are not good enough. One trouble is the exceptions and the restrictions. Even the Ten Commandments and other rules have been applied only to a limited area of behavior. The ancients said: "You may not steal from your neighbor if he is part of your group or family, but it is all right to steal from him if he is not. If he is a person across the ravine or down the river, you can take his cattle and slaves, and it is all right to kill him too." With differences only in degree, we have been saying much the same thing ever since.

The codes have been restricted also in terms of the parties involved. For example, centuries ago it was agreed that the nobility were an exception. It was all right to violate the commandments if you were a king or a lord. In England until only a few hundred years ago the man in the castle on the hill could do what he wanted with lesser people; he could enclose their land for his own purposes, conscript their labor, or take their wives. Around 1789 in Europe, according to Joseph Barry, the seigneur of the manor was authorized in certain cantons "to have two of his vassals disembowelled on his return from the hunt, so that he might refresh his feet in their warm bodies."[15]

Another big exception has been made for the state. How many millions of people have been killed because the state ordered it? Violence from that source has always been accepted as valid. In fact, the debate over the treatment of dissenters and objectors to the Vietnam war has made it perfectly clear that many legislators and government officials feel that *not* to kill is an unforgivable sin, at least when a person is ordered to do so by the government. Thousands of years of precedent are on their side. It was all right for Christians to kill or steal from the Saracens because the Saracens had the wrong religion. It was all right for the English to kill the natives of India—the government said so, and besides, it was agreed that the natives were a lesser breed. In this country it was all right for our ancestors to kill American Indians—the federal and state governments all agreed on this. Until a century or so ago it was all right for a Southern landowner to kill blacks—as long as they were his own.

The Christian church, too, has been excepted from the rules. For centuries the church said that it was all right to kill heretics. They could be burned at the stake because they were wrong. Whenever the pope found an enemy of God and the church, he could issue a bull authorizing anyone to hunt down that enemy and kill him. Not only was it all right but the killer would receive special awards in heaven for his deed. When Mussolini's armed forces left to destroy the Ethiopians in 1935, a representative of the papacy blessed the government's instruments of warfare.

What about husbands and fathers? Traditionally a husband could be violent with his wife and children. Only today are strictures being put on this age-old liberty, and we are having a difficult time getting the public to accept the limitations. The "battered child" is a common occurrence in every community, and little is done to prevent it. Children are still treated as possessions even as blacks were in the age of slavery.

The Ten Commandments and other codes have not applied where the motivation for violence has been considered justifiable. Generally, of course, this means that an agency of government or the church must be involved, though not always, as in the case of what the law has called "justifiable homicide." Murderers, traitors, and others can be shot, hanged, beheaded, or gassed by the state if it decides that this is necessary to maintain law and order. If you watched the Democratic National Convention in Chicago in 1968, you saw Mayor Richard Daley's security forces bludgeoning protesters; that was legal, too, because it was done in the name of law and order.

But "law and order" is not the only motivation that justifies violence in the world today. In the 1930's Stalin could kill millions of kulaks not because they threatened physical harm but in order to teach the Russian people a lesson about Communism. Our own country has used a similar technique, has it not? For instance, the sudden bombing of North Vietnam, late in the war, to teach Hanoi a lesson when it threatened to upset negotiations in progress. The French separatists in Quebec, the Palestinian Independents, the Symbionese Liberation Army—these organizations, too, have used violence in order to impress their opponents. In 1974, on the sixtieth anniversary of the assassination of Archduke Franz Ferdinand and his wife Sophie (the event precipitating World War I), it was reported that the Communist party in Yugoslavia gave its tacit blessing to the production of a movie portraying the plotters as heroes. Communist party leaders are only "troubled" by the problem of whether assassination was justified as a political tool.[16] It is no wonder that Aleksandr Solzhenitsyn, noting acts like these, was inspired to write:

> Violence, continually less restrained by the confines of a legality established over the course of many generations,

strides brazenly and victoriously through the whole world, unconcerned with the fact that its sterility has already been manifested and proven many times in history. Nor is it merely brute force that triumphs but its trumpeted justification also: the whole world is being flooded with the crude conviction that force can do everything and righteousness and innocence nothing. Dostoyevsky's DEVILS, who seemed a provincial, nightmarish fantasy of the last century, are crawling under our very eyes through the whole world.[17]

While I do not agree with Solzhenitsyn that violence has been held in check in the past, I concur that it is spreading and intensifying. It is important to understand that this development is not happenstance or coincidence but the result of certain trends and forces with predictable impacts. Let us look at them briefly.

First, we are in the midst of an epochal crisis, with transformations occurring in our culture, economy, family life, and community life. Whenever people are shaken and disturbed, they tend to revert. Placed under unusual stress and strain, the nicest man or woman may suddenly erupt in violence, because for millions of years violence was bred into human nature. Let us not forget that! However much we pride ourselves on our civilization, it has had small impact on human nature compared with the millennia of jungle destruction and cannibalism.

Second, a time of confusion, change, and seeming emptiness brings out the necrophiles. These are the people who have a stronger death wish than most of us have; they love life less. (The opposite of necrophile is biophile, a term for the person who glorifies life.) As Erich Fromm has observed, the necrophile doesn't care whom he hurts—the victim is incidental.[18] Such Nazis as Eichmann and Goebbels were necrophiles, and it is not accidental that they used such symbols as skulls and death's-heads on helmets. I would apply the term also to the law-and-order enthusiasts who glorify troops and surveillance as a means of wiping out dissidence. Fromm calls the violence of a necrophile "compensatory," meaning that it is used to make up for life's lack of love and enjoyment. He states:

> Compensatory violence is not something superficial, the result of evil influences, bad habits, and so on. It is a power in man as intense and strong as his wish to live. It is so strong precisely because it constitutes the revolt of life against its being crippled; man has a potential for destructive and sadistic violence because he is human, because he is not a thing, and because he must try to destroy life if he cannot create it.[19]

A third trend is the increase in population and the multiplying rules, restrictions, and frictions in densely populated communities. We rub and bump against each other all the time. After containing a certain amount of irritation, resentment, and frustration, we blow up. Moreover, injustices are more easily overlooked in this age of heavy population—except by the ones who get hurt. The latter become resentful, and this usually leads to violence.

A fourth trend is the decline of neighborliness. We live in neighborhoods but have no neighbors. Little concerned about those who live close to us, we don't feel that the traditional codes apply to our relationships with them. A person on the other side of a thin wall is not considered to be part of us—he's a stranger, so why shouldn't we take what we want from him? The more conglomerate a neighborhood, the greater the likelihood of violence. A gang need only go to the next street to find itself in an alien area.

The tragedy is that our feeling of community has eroded just when we need it most. If we know what it is to care for a relative or neighbor, we gain some kind of protection against the jungle; the ties that bind, however few, form a shelter and a learning experience. But how are we to learn to care for one another if our families don't stay together, or if we uproot ourselves so often that we never develop strong relationships with neighbors? If we never learn how to love, then everybody around is prey. This danger is what drives many young people to find community groups with bonds of some sort, however unusual, that enable them to feel a sense of brotherhood. They want something to hold on to.

Finally, violence is done to us by those who would love us. If our parents, relatives, and teachers do not feel loved, they have little love to give children. In the name of love, children are constrained and controlled to suit their elders' desires. The children react predictably. Lack of love corrupts; those deprived learn to use love as a tool of aggression and depredation of others. This is why R. D. Laing warns that we are destroying one another by "violence masquerading as love." Laing explains:

> From the moment of birth, when the Stone Age baby confronts the twentieth-century mother, the baby is subjected to these forces of violence, called love, as its mother and father, and their parents and their parents before them, have been. These forces are mainly concerned with destroying most of its potentialities, and on the whole this enterprise is successful. By the time the new human being is fifteen or so, we are left with a being like ourselves, half-crazed creature more or less adjusted to a mad world. This is normality in our present age.[20]

Principles and Approaches

The five trends and forces described are prevalent and strong—and are becoming more so. Yet the day for violence is done. We live too closely to afford violence as primitive peoples could. We have to find ways to live together in peace because we can no longer get away from one another, even when separated by oceans. Matthew describes how Jesus spoke to crowds after receiving questions from John the Baptist, then in prison. "From the days of John the Baptist until now," Jesus said, "the kingdom of heaven has suffered violence, and men of violence take it by force." (Matt. 11:12.) Violence was all right once upon a time, but no longer. We cannot survive with hateful people around. No one has a right to use violence; no motive justifies violence. It is an anticommunity force, antievolutionary, anti-Godly. We must find ways to apply the codes used by loving families to whole communities, regions, nations, and the world.

I offer the following principles and approaches for those who want to check and reduce violence in society.

1. *We can change the conditions that foment violence.* It doesn't do much good to ask, "Who's to blame for all this?" No one is to blame. The economic, social, cultural, educational, family, genetic, and other conditions that lead one person to become violent could also turn you or me to violence. It is significant, I think, that any sociologist can go into any city, get a map of it, ascertain facts about certain conditions, and tell you without exploring the statistics on crime where the acts of violence take place. He can tell you the kinds of crimes committed in this area or that, and he can tell

you in general the relationship of those crimes to other criminal acts.

The influence of conditions on crime is enormous. The last time I gathered some comparisons in Grand Rapids, for instance, two contiguous districts possessing contrasting socioeconomic conditions showed these differences for the most recent period: 8 murders in one to none in the other; 5 rapes in one to none in the other; 68 robberies in one to none in the other; 35 assault cases to 1 in the other; 297 burglaries to 39; 605 larcenies to 200; 151 auto thefts to 12. Here is another example: A study several years ago showed that while reported crimes in the Queens area of New York City were climbing at a rate of 12.5 percent, those in one part of the area, Maspeth (the 112th precinct), were declining more than 10 percent. In this stable neighborhood, few residents had complicated locks on their homes, few stores had iron gates, and the children played peacefully. Yet conditions were just the opposite in the communities around Maspeth.[21]

What can we do? Let me mention a few possibilities. We can provide for adequate professional services for delinquent children. Adult offenders are often beyond the pale of effective rehabilitation, but we can have unbounded faith and hope in the possibilities of guiding children to responsible behavior. We can improve living conditions in areas infested with rats, mice, and insects. We can invest in better schools. We can do more to assure that parents who want to work can find decent jobs and provide for their families. We can revolutionize a system of courts, conviction procedures, and prisons that today do more to manufacture crime, penologists believe, than abate it. Ramsey Clark, one of our most respected authorities on this subject, makes this indictment of the present system:

Ninety-five cents of every dollar spent in the entire corrections effort in the United States is for custody: iron bars, stone walls, guards. The remaining five cents of that dollar is for hope: health service, education, developing employment skills.[22]

2. *We can give more adequate support to urban police forces.* In numerous U.S. cities, police departments are maintained at inadequate levels, and too often they appear to be manipulated for political purposes. We need to increase salaries and facilities, not to hold the line, in most cases. That is going to increase the tax rate, of course, but it is an important way of coping with the problem. And we need to be more helpful to the police. In most cases this simply means giving them a telephone call when we see something that looks suspicious; in a few instances it may mean going further than that, as when a business tries to prevent inroads by organized crime.

If we do not provide the local police with the help they need in order to do the job of preventing violence, what is the alternative? It is to employ the military to keep law and order. We Americans are not going to let the high rates of murder, mugging, rape, burglary, and other crimes continue unabated in our cities. Shall we give local law-enforcement officers the means to cope, or in desperation shall we become a military state?

3. *We must not only allow but encourage peaceful protest.* We must open up more avenues for the expression of nonviolent revolt against our wastes of money, our neglect of people, our laws that discriminate, our bureaucracies that become self-serving rather than public-serving, our schemes to control other nations. This means giving more, not less, freedom to dissident groups to do such things as:

Use public parks for demonstration

March through the central business district at commuting hour

Arrange confrontation meetings with public officials

Wear clothes and hairstyles that offend the majority taste (at religious worship as well as at daily work in business, government, and other organizations)

Distribute propagandistic leaflets up and down the main thoroughfares

Excoriate "the establishment" in student newspapers and employee publications

Use valuable television and radio time to present dissident viewpoints

Organize and participate freely in forums, debates, and public discussions in churches, town halls, and other buildings where public meetings are generally held

Opening the way for more protests and peaceful dissidence is not a popular solution, and there are risks involved. For instance, this approach may produce litter in the parks, embarrassment to mayors and corporate leaders, lost sales, minor fights, and other difficulties. Moreover, dissident groups are prone to exaggeration, immaturity, and distortion of the facts. How then is this policy to be defended? The case might be put this way:

The only valid way to suppress unwanted demonstrations is to make demonstrations legitimate. And the only way to have them legitimate is to run the risk of having them illegitimate! To have peaceful dissent we must expose ourselves to the danger of angry dissent getting out of hand. Otherwise there is no law as we in the United States and other Western countries have come to understand it; there is only law as a brutal form of violence itself, in the sense that it forcefully prevents freedom of choice for those who disagree with the parties in power.

The real danger is that our fear of the radical will goad us to compromise democratic principles; in our horror of chaos and upsetting changes we may impulsively turn to "strong" public officials who will prevent the disorderliness. Freedom and danger go together. Protest is not "pretty" or "nice." But the risk that peaceful demonstrations will result in civil disorder, public inconvenience, and property damage is acceptable, whereas the risk of blundering into a form of police state is not.

4. *We must persuade through "power in personality."* Violence never persuades. When Germany and Japan surrendered at the end of World War II, they were not persuaded that militarism was wrong. We had to go to those nations and bind up the wounds, restore the shattered threads of economic, social, and political dependency. Only in that way could we hope to remove some of the hatred, antagonism, and resentment from the hearts of those peoples (and from our own hearts). In short, when the war was over we had to go back to the beginning and start again, doing what we might earlier have done if we had not lost the opportunity because of ignorance, impatience, and brutality.

Similarly, when the Civil War ended we had not achieved concern in the North and South for the ties that bound the states together. We were farther from that achievement in 1865 than at the beginning of the war because of the antagonisms and bitterness aroused by military violence. We had to begin persuading without the use of force. More than a hundred years later we are still involved in that effort at persuasion. The war was necessary but it did not, by itself, change Southerners' thinking about our federal form of government.

When our children anger and annoy us, revealing our weaknesses as parents as well as their weaknesses as children, we may spank them. But every parent knows that violent punishment does not persuade children. It may bring an end to their hostility or irritating behavior, but all it teaches them is that in the future they may again be punished for such and such violations. If we seek to persuade our children, we must find a way to reach their hatred, resentment, hurt pride, or sense of injustice so that the power of love can work.

However attractive violence may seem to us, and however necessary in moments of extremity, it is a form of power that cultured people no longer can afford to use. Marshall McLuhan observes: "When men are subdued by force, they do not submit in their minds, but only because their strength is inadequate. When men are subdued by power in personality, they are pleased to their very heart's core, and they do really submit."[23] Every religious leader of any significance or merit, even though he lived in a barbaric time, has understood the truth of this statement.

Part of the genius of Jesus was his dependence on the qualities of persuasion, his rejection of any kind of temptation (and there were many temptations, as always for men of strength) to exercise his power through violence. He could be sharp with people and "upbraid the cities where most of his mighty works had been done" (Matt. 11:20), but he insisted on the approach that the only way for people to see God and to understand themselves in the light of God was through nonviolent persuasion. He knew that love does not respond to and cannot win with violence.

The same understanding belonged to the great Chinese prophet, Lao-tzu. Poetically he described "the way" of quietness, gentleness, hiddenness, mystery, love—the power that does not crush. And the great Indian prophet and saint, Buddha, tried to find the way to people's hearts through loving understanding of themselves and the world.

In our own time, the power of persuasion was epitomized by Gandhi. This strange and wonderful genius who has towered over this century as have few men in history turned an empire back without force (except as it arose on the outskirts of his movement). Not a Christian, yet understanding Christianity, he talked to men and women through their ideas, ideals, and hopes in such a way that they came to understand the nature of the social structure. He knew the time had come for the British to understand the Indians and for the Indians to find their freedom. The British wiped out many people with guns and bombs, but Gandhi had faith that his approach would work—and that if it did not work today, it would work tomorrow.

Martin Luther King, Jr., tried the same way. This great preacher from a Southern Baptist church knew that force could not destroy and win at the same time. Nonviolent protest was his way to the hearts of both whites and Negroes. He taught through simple demonstration of the validity of man's ancient faith in brotherhood. His approach worked, and it goes on working.

Leaders such as these illustrate the power of personality and persuasion. Their techniques are unimportant; their principles are important. Persuasion calls for grown-up people and does not work in the hands of imitators and frauds, who turn us away because we know they are manipulating. The absurd man with a beard and ragged clothes who, supposing himself to be another Gandhi, gets himself imprisoned and goes on a hunger strike, and in other ways imitates the Indian leader—this person is not the kind I am writing about. Nor is the person who burns himself or herself to death in the streets, as the Buddhists did in the streets of Saigon during the 1960's.

Worse even than the imitators are those who mouth the words of nonviolence in order to disarm people. The Student Nonviolent Coordinating Committee, which was organized before King's assassination, is an example. It used the label "nonviolent" as a tactic—in actuality it had few qualms about using violence. I once heard its young leader say on a television program that the device of nonviolence could be dropped any time it was convenient. To my way of thinking, he represented either extreme ignorance or venality at its worst. I do not say that violence may not sometimes be necessary in these mixed-up times; what I do say is that no person should proceed to use it, even in the most urgent circumstances, without breaking his or her heart over the necessity.

CHAPTER 8

Dishonesty

Dishonesty could be called the unpardonable sin. The four sins described earlier—ignorance, arrogance, greed, and violence—are natural and unavoidable. We can hold them in check but they are so basic that we cannot get away from them. However, dishonesty is a conscious act, a deliberate effort to cheat and distort. It is a repudiation of the validity of life itself, because it implies a refusal to go along with reality. By lying or misrepresenting, we change the real world into an unreal world. We destroy the possibilities for creativity, we obfuscate the goodness of God, we go against that which is basic to our humanity and our hopes. Jesus condemned what he called the "hypocrites," identifying them to a large degree with Pharisees. "But woe to you, scribes and Pharisees, hypocrites! because you shut the kingdom of heaven against men; for you neither enter yourselves, nor allow those who would enter to go in." (Matt. 23:13.)

One morning a friend left on my desk a cartoon called "Animal Crackers." It showed two leaders out in front of a column of people marching—the column was so long that it disappeared in the distance. One leader was saying to the other, "I think honesty is the best policy, so you tell them in a calm, steady voice that we haven't the slightest idea where we are." This is a beautiful insight into the problems of honesty. I have asked a number of critical people who like to discuss issues to tell me about dishonesty. "What do you think about it?" I asked. Invariably each person hesitated, paused, and answered with words such as: "Well, I don't really know. I'm not sure how to deal with it." I was asking them because I had the same general feeling. The trouble is that dishonesty is so pervasive. It is almost inconceivable that we could eliminate it, and so in the face of an overwhelming situation we shrug and feel helpless.

In a recent television speech a politician stated, "No one in government these days can be trusted." How many times has this statement been echoed in media all over the land? At San Francisco in 1974 the president of the American Association for the Advancement of Science made this statement on the dangers that face us: "Recent manifestations of encroaching danger include the rise of government 'doublespeak' in which real problems are obscured or declared solved by semantic tricks and where attempts are made to rewrite history by denying bombing raids or distorting copies of cables." Such practices have been confirmed again and again.

In a public opinion survey I saw recently, Americans were queried about the amount of trust they had in the honesty of people in sixteen professions and institutions. The medical profession rated highest—with 54 percent professing faith in it. Hardly more than half! Science and scientists came in second, with only 37 percent of the respondents believing them to be trustworthy. Religion? The officials of this institution, which should rank high—at least in honesty—were fifth, far below science and medicine. The executive branch of the Federal Government? Our top leaders in Washington came in tenth. Congress fared even worse, ranking twelfth on the list of the sixteen. As for the press—on which we are so dependent for information about what is going on in the country and community —it ranked thirteenth. Television, labor, and advertising completed the bottom of the list.

In the early 1960's, when the Kennedy Administration was alleging inadequacies in the U.S. atomic missile defense, the term "credibility gap" was originated. Gerald Ford, then a congressman, is credited with first using the term. It was associated with government at first, but today it is applied everywhere. An advertiser told me: "I am commissioned to write an ad for a local business. The company wants me to head the ad, 'Sale. Sale. Sale, Giant Sale!' I ask, 'How much are you reducing your price, or what are you giving as an extra?' They answer, 'Nothing.' So I ask, 'Then how can we call it a sale?' They reply, 'You call it a sale because that's the way we want it advertised.' "

A commission established by Congress has been investigating packaging for several years. It has compiled a long list of ways in which consumers are deceived—false bottoms in cartons, jars labeled "Giant Economy Size" that actually cost more per ounce than smaller-size jars do, and so on. Many such deceptions have been ended, as a result of the commission's work, but no careful shopper needs to be told that misrepresentations are still common.

The chicanery of car salesmen and repairmen is so notorious that it is the butt of countless jokes—dishonesty in this area is practically accepted as part of the American way! And not too long ago I saw an advertisement for a new book entitled *How to Steal.* The publisher declared that here was your chance to get back at all those who had been gouging you over the years. The author reportedly described ways to steal almost everything you can imagine.

How did American and other Western societies get to be this way? The history of dishonesty must be as ancient as the history of communications, but I believe that many roots of the practice are in recent times. Hitler would have to be a major influence. His gigantic deceptions to the German people and the world, his philosophy that the bigger the lie the more apt it is to be believed, his falsehoods about his ancestry and that of the German people, his lies about the Jews, his dictates about what results scientists should produce— these and many other acts of dishonesty had effects which, I believe, are still with us. Stalin did the same thing in the Soviet Union, twisting facts and scientific evidence to get results that would help him lead millions of people in the direction he wanted to go.

United States leaders have contributed their share too. There is considerable historical evidence now to indicate that President Franklin D. Roosevelt deceived us grossly in order to get this nation involved in World War II. I do not say that we should not have entered the war, only that we did not make a free choice to enter it because of his manipulation of information. Many of us remember vividly Senator Joseph McCarthy of Wisconsin waving lists of so-called proved Communists in government—486 such people, he claimed in a Wheeling, West Virginia, speech. The horrible lies that he used to stir up the nation did so much damage that we still suffer from it. Consider the enormity of McCarthy's claim that General George C. Marshall, rated by many top authorities (including Winston Churchill) as one of the greatest Americans of all time, was the

Soviet Union's chief representative in this country seeking to establish Communism in the United States! That lie was believed by many people, because in true Hitler style it was proclaimed loudly and often.

Even our heroes have lied to us. There was President Dwight D. Eisenhower, who deliberately and openly lied that our Air Force had not authorized any surveillance planes to fly over the Soviet Union. There was General Douglas MacArthur, who, as chief of staff in the Far East, grossly misrepresented (and later apologized for) what was happening during the Korean war. There was Martin Luther King, Jr., who deceived his followers and all of us in that historic confrontation at the bridge in Selma. Before the parade began, King worked out an agreement with the government: at a precise point after crossing the bridge, he would be confronted, whereupon he would confer with the government officials and then disband the parade. King did not have the honesty to tell his people about that agreement. There were generals and admirals in charge of our forces in the Vietnam war who concealed the truth from visiting dignitaries touring South Vietnam, falsified reports going to Defense Secretary Robert McNamara and Secretary of State Dean Rusk, and misled the press. When the top officials in Washington became involved in the deception, *they* did not have the courage to reverse themselves. Much of the Government was caught up in a maelstrom of dishonesty. All but two senators voted for the Tonkin Gulf resolution because the evidence presented to them was so distorted. Many who voted for it have since apologized, admitted their mistake, and accepted the resulting shame and embarrassment.

Do we have to say much about Watergate? Whatever else we may believe about that sorry series of episodes, one thing that comes through loud and clear is the continuous, extensive, and often systematized amount of lying that went on. But was it all the fault of those involved in the cover-up? Could they have operated that way without considerable support and acceptance of what they were doing?

This is what I find so troubling, that we *accept* as much dishonesty as we do. For it is impossible to live creatively on lies, deception, misrepresentation, and hypocrisy. Honesty is not important for animals, but it is essential for humanity: *We have to know what we are dealing with.* If a person changes the appearance of his behavior, motives, products, or company in order to manipulate us, so that we deal with an illusion instead of reality, we are done in. And if in retaliation we do the same thing, we are on the way to turning human relationship into a farce. We die from taking a bottle labeled medicine that is really poison.

Our civilization was built on the basis of the scientific method, which is a way to confirm truth and distinguish it from fiction, to make sure that purported facts are real and not the product of someone's fancy or crusading zeal. Whether we like it or not, civilization as we know it could never have been produced without the benefit of the scientific approach. How can we deal productively with nature if nature is misrepresented to us? How can a company do business if it cannot count on the promises, commitments, and statements of suppliers, buyers, and contractors? How can a neighborhood be happy if the people in it lie to one another?

In ancient times members of a tribe lived face-to-face, and in that kind of relationship there was a discipline that made honesty enforceable. But in the world today we do not have that discipline. We are dependent on sources of information we cannot check back on, and if they deceive us, we may not learn that until too late. A society without honesty is going to end up in paralysis, with the individual not knowing how to behave because of suspicion and fear, trying to protect himself with a phalanx of attorneys in order to obtain valid understandings and agreements. Out of that comes frustration, then comes suspicion and armed-camp hostility, and finally violence destroying everything.

I believe that our civilization cannot endure much longer with as much dishonesty as there is now. What is the solution? I have no answers. We have a problem that we and our children must work with for years to come—that much is sure—and I can only offer some suggestions to stimulate more thinking.

First, we must pay more attention to the dangers of dishonesty. We must be more aware of how vulnerable we are. Since we cannot enjoy face-to-face relationships with our heads of state, legislators, military leaders, television officials, and others who package information for us, we have to depend on them to handle their relationships with us with integrity. Our dependency is increased because events move so rapidly. There is no time to investigate dishonesty, as there was in the nineteenth century; we find out about it too late to save ourselves. I see no alternative to this dependence; my point is that we must be more awake to the dangers of it.

Second, we can practice honesty in our relationships in the family, community, church, and at work. Even if much of society is moving in the other direction, we can start local reversals of the trend, and these droplets could merge into a wave that someday would change society.

Next, we can demand honesty more often from our leaders and institutional officials. When we feel we are not getting it from them, change them! We cannot

afford to let matters drift, to wait for improvement to
come from initiatives on the other side. Some moral
fervor is essential for this cause.

Finally, we must be willing to pay the price of
honesty. When we know a teacher who has the courage
to be honest, we can support him or her even though
the truth that comes out makes our neighbors and us
feel uncomfortable. We can support the politician who
is honest even though he or she is abrasive or favors a
policy we do not like. Honesty has become more important than intellectual brilliance in public life! We can
support and encourage the preacher who is honest—
too many preachers work in communities that prefer
comfort to honesty. We can encourage the employee
who is honest with us during working hours, even
though his or her honesty hurts us.

The Lesser Sin of Too Much Honesty

As noted in Chapter 2, the opposite of a sin is not
always a virtue. Dishonesty and honesty are a case in
point. In thinking about the need to improve honesty
in behavior and communications, we can profit from
an awareness of the shortcomings of complete, absolute honesty. It is in this spirit that I suggest seven
exceptions, in ascending order of importance, to the
maxim that "honesty is the best policy."

1. *Honesty may spoil the game.* If we are playing
cards, we don't want to know what the other person
holds. In many foreign marketplaces, bargaining and
price haggling with predictable overemphasis or un-
deremphasis on the value of a product is an enjoyable
part of the cultural and community life. Another example is management-union bargaining in the United
States: An expert on this process tells me that many
owners make the mistake of assuming that all they

have to do is be completely honest with their employees at bargaining time. So they throw their cards
on the table. "Here's how much money I have. Spread
it around. Do with it whatever you want." Now, the
owner's motivation may be good, the expert explains,
but bargaining is a game and the game is spoiled when
this approach is taken. For wage bargaining is a peculiar relationship involving people from opposite sides
who are trying to find a mutually acceptable middle
ground. When the owner takes the position described,
he says, in effect, "This is the end of the dialogue." It
is a kind of ultimatum, leaving labor representatives
with no place to go and causing them to lose face with
their constituents. Conversation is shut off, and, with
it, opportunities for growth in understanding and
creativity.

2. *Honesty may be an intrusion.* When people say to
me, "You don't look very well," they may be honest but
they can also be intruding in my private sphere. I have
a space around me that is important to me; not everyone is invited into that space. My point is that the pass-
erby, casual acquaintance, and even close friend
should be wary of going in where not invited, though
they do so in the name of honesty.

This is generally true when we use the word
"should." "You should not do that—you can't afford it."
Or, "You should find time to read this book." Or, "You
should tell your children not to act that way." Why do
we feel driven so often to talk this way? Perhaps it is
because we get so much in the habit of giving our
children restrictions necessary for health and safety
that unconsciously we begin treating adults the same
way. Perhaps the drug problem—including alcohol
abuse—could be handled better if we did not try so
hard to tell users what they "should" do. Might they not
have a right to go to hell in their own way? In short,

honesty is not a sufficiently perfect virtue to justify the *imposition* of our beliefs and judgments on others.

3. *Honesty may be used as a weapon for hurting people.* When possible, evil uses what appear to be good motives to achieve its ends. For example, there is the telephone call to a wife about her husband, or to a husband about his wife—where the caller saw the spouse, and with whom, and doing what. Is the call really for the listener's own good? Or does the caller do it for his or her own delight? You may be able to hear the pleasure in the caller's voice and manner of recounting. The eagerness to tell, the disappointment if the listener does not gasp with dismay! "I was only trying to help," the caller says. "I just want to be honest with you. I'd want to know if I were in your position, and I'm sure you'd want to know."

4. *Honesty may be a ploy for self-defense.* "If I tell you what I did, it will be all right, won't it—because I was honest?" How early our children learn to come to us with statements like this! When we get angry at the revelation, they have their defense ready: "Well, you said I should tell you the truth, didn't you?" We incorporate this maneuver into our legal system, granting certain immunities to criminals if they tell us the truth, so that we can then convict others. Their honesty is rewarded even though it is a betrayal of others.

In my observation, practically every adult has learned this art of self-defense. By relating exactly what happened in one area, we assure that there will not be too much examination of *why* it happened or of what our just deserts really are. The whole point of honesty and self-inquiry then becomes lost in gamesmanship.

5. *Honesty may be a form of self-gratification.* We may dump our burdens of guilt on people who cannot carry them. We think it would be great if they could see

us as we are—know the sin we have committed. "Well, I've been honest, open, and aboveboard," we go away thinking. The trouble is that the person dumped upon may not have the kind of mind that can rid itself of the burden, so that now he or she won't be able to see us again without thinking of the vice or crime described. This is why Alcoholics Anonymous says to the alcoholic who is on the way back and wants to live a constructive life, "If you've done harm to anybody, you should go back and make amends *if* by making amends you will not further hurt that person." The hurt you gave originally may be manageable, but bringing it up again with the person may arouse hostilities and resentments that cannot be managed.

We need to be able to tell people about problems that bother us—after all, even the pope has a confessor. But we must do this with restraint, keeping in mind the delicacy of human relationships as well as our motives in "telling all."

6. *People are not always ready for the truth.* For instance, experts on sex education urge us to answer a child's question about sex, and answer it honestly, but without feeling that we have to tell the child everything we know. The child may not be ready for that much information yet. When he or she gets ready for a further question, he'll ask it. Similarly, a dying person may not want to be told. I believe that I have known no one in a lingering terminal illness who did not realize what was going on. But I have seen few who wanted me or others to tell them about it. If they did, they asked.

Much harm is done by those of us who blunder in thinking that others should be as strong and honest as we are. Many are not able to take the truth. They may be too weak to stand too much of it, no matter how trivial; they may be barely able to hold on in cruel and harsh circumstances. Their dreams and fantasies may be essential to keep them going, and telling them too much of the truth may break down their protection.

7. *Our capacity for honesty is limited.* Theoretically we should be perfectly open with those we love intimately; there should be "nothing between us." But very few of us can stand that much candor. I have learned to warn my friends about the dangers of "honesty groups" where people sit around and tell each other exactly what they think and feel. Sooner or later they will get so hurt that they will be unable to be as honest as they were before they started. In short, there are many lines and limits in human relationships, and it is important to respect them. Many married people have found that even after many years of marriage there are some things which perhaps they should be able to manage but cannot really. If the relationship is a good one, the partner respects such weaknesses, needs, and uncertainties. If complete honesty might destroy a sound and happy relationship, is it really a virtue?

There are some things that can be said in a business relationship that cannot be said in a social relationship, and there are things that cannot be said in a marriage that can be said in a friendship. The type of relationship is obviously important.

Oliver Wendell Holmes once said, "Sin has many tools, but a lie is the handle which fits them all." Dishonesty is a deadly sin. Its opposite, honesty, is an imperfect ideal. The need is to accept these somewhat conflicting realities, recognizing that the end objective is growth and creativity. Several years ago I offered a prayer that sums up the purpose of this chapter:

"Let it be our prayer that we will have such a community of those who care that we will be able to be honest with ourselves and with each other. Let it be our prayer that our community and the ties of love that bind us together will be so enriching that we will have the courage to be what we feel we ought to be, say the things that are on our minds, and act in accord with our beliefs and understandings. Let it be our prayer that we will have such strength and depth of loving relationships that we will be able to accept the differences that exist between us and find the courage to live in confidence with each other—in our community, our nation, and the whole world."

CHAPTER 9

Indifference

Life is involvement. We struggle coming into it, we struggle to endure on the way through it, and we struggle going out of it. It is fight or flight all the way. It is impossible to live in this kind of world without being involved in the problems of how to avoid destruction and achieve some of our needs, hopes, and ideals. Love and hate dictate much of what we do. We move toward some things and away from others. We desire certain qualities and despise others. We fight for some things and against others.

What is the great enemy of life? It is not hatred, because we can continue to love while hating. Indeed, the two are close together, since they result from feelings of care and concern. The real enemy is apathy and indifference; these qualities are the true opposites of love. The great betrayal of life is not to be involved in it. In the vast distances and huge agglomerations of material in the universe, only this planet supports complex life—so far as we know. Not to care about this precious process, not to be absorbed in it, not to be involved in the struggle for growth and fulfillment—surely this is a negation of God and a deadly sin.

Many close and careful observers of the human scene have expressed similar convictions. The poet T. S. Eliot writes:

> There are three conditions which often look alike
> Yet differ completely, flourish in the same hedgerow:
> Attachment to self and to things and to persons, detachment
> From self and from things and from persons; and, growing
> between them, indifference
> Which resembles the others as death resembles life.[24]

Rollo May, a great and insightful psychologist, has made numerous statements in support of the point. Here is but one example: "The most tragic thing of all in the long run is the ultimate attitude, 'It doesn't matter.' "[25] And Arthur Janov, another insightful psychologist, who bases his whole approach on the importance of feeling and expressing feelings, states that the most disastrous feeling a little child can have is that there is no one who cares. The child "cannot live knowing that he is despised or that no one is really interested in him."[26] How many lives have been ruined because of the belief that no one cares? One may have great knowledge, riches, and physical comfort, "yet the light of a whole life dies when love is done."[27] Here are some observations by Karl Menninger:

> Both believers and skeptics are people of minds, people of hearts, people who are trying to understand themselves and their fellow men and the world in which they all live. Their real opposition—the common enemy . . . is the complacency of the comfortable. It is the indifference, the apathy, the hardness of heart which troubles neither to believe nor to doubt, but simply does not care.[28]

One of the major figures of our time in the area of understanding personality and quality of life is the late Abraham Maslow. He is the author of this statement:

> By protecting himself against the hell within himself, he [man] also cuts himself off from the heaven within. In the extreme instance, we have the obsessional person, flat, tight, rigid, frozen, controlled, cautious, who can't laugh or play or love or be silly or trusting or childish.[29]

In a fascinating book on concentration camps, Viktor Frankl shows that the people who come through best are those who have a dream. The possessor of a dream can hold on through the pit of hell. The people who do not come through are those who do not care, withdrawing so much into themselves that they become rigid, insensitive zombies shut off from everything around them. Frankl says that one could actually see such a withdrawal happening; day by day the person retreated further into himself, until finally nothing mattered and it was impossible for anyone to get through to him, even with pain.[30]

The Bible depicts vividly the evil of indifference. There was Pharaoh, whose heart was hardened and who could not hear the laments and wailing of the Jewish people or the pleadings of Moses. But if Pharaoh sinned by being indifferent, so did the Jews themselves, and God promises Ezekiel that he "will take the stony heart out of their flesh and give them a heart of flesh" (Ezek. 11:19). Again, when God was about to destroy the city of Sodom for its sins, Abraham implored him not to. "Now if there are fifty good people there, will you spare the city?" Abraham asked, and God said yes. "If only forty, would you spare it, God?" And so on, until Abraham got him down to just ten good people in the city. "Would you spare it even then, God?" Again the answer was yes. (Gen. 18:22–32.)

The Book of Jonah contains perhaps the most beautiful story of caring. Mention Jonah to most people and they think of a man swallowed by a whale and cast up on shore again, but that miracle is incidental to the story. Jonah was picked out by God to go to the city of Nineveh to tell the people how sinful they were —so wicked that God had had enough of them and was going to destroy them. Being somewhat of a necrophile, Jonah enjoyed telling the people what terrible destruction lay ahead of them. In fact, he warned them so effectively that they reformed. From the king on down, they repented of their sins and resolved that they would henceforth be obedient to the will of God. Then God in his mercy forgave them and told Jonah he would not destroy the city. Jonah was so incensed over these wicked people being pardoned that he pleaded with God to let him die rather than witness this travesty of justice. But God was not swayed. He asked, "Should not I pity Nineveh, that great city, in which there are more than a hundred and twenty thousand persons who do not know their right hand from their left, and also much cattle?" (Jonah 4:11.)

Then there was Jesus, who spent much effort countering the hardness of heart of even his closest followers. He repudiated them for turning away from a crippled man. He healed the sick, comforted the bruised, tended to the afflicted. Jesus' personality was full of caring. The story of the crucifixion is basically a story of caring. God gave his only-begotten son in expiation of the sins of man. No matter how evil, sinful, and destructive man becomes, God holds on and continues to care. This is the story of our religion.

How extensive is indifference in our society? In my observation a great many Americans are drifting into a state of physical comfort, lack of feeling, and emotional insulation from the cries and laments of others in the community. Our playwrights and dramatists have been sensitive to this drift. In *The Iceman Cometh,* Eugene O'Neill's vision of the desperation of nothingness, the bartender keeps repeating, "Who cares?" In Arthur Miller's *Death of a Salesman* the sons seem indifferent to the fate of their father. They are chastized by their mother: "You know, he's not an animal. He may not be a great person, but he's a person. He's a human being, and something terrible is happening to him. Attention must be paid."

One of the most penetrating depictions of this trend that I have found is in a small and little-known book by H. G. Wells called *The Croquet Player.*[31] Significantly, it came out in 1938, while the Western nations were passively watching Hitler expand his power. Toward the end of the novel a psychiatrist is explaining a case of strange behavior to a young man who is one of the central characters. Refusing to face a world as grim as it really is, the psychiatrist says, some sensitive people try to run away from reality. But the facts must be faced, the psychiatrist insists, and one of these is that people are essentially the same fearing, snarling, fighting cavemen they were hundreds of thousands of years ago. The young man asks what has to be done. The psychiatrist's answer is that those who care for civilization must become giants who will make an enormous effort to build a harder, stronger, more disciplined society. While he is explaining, the young man keeps pulling away. The young man feels nervous and frightened over all this apocalyptic talk. Finally he cries that he realizes the world is going to pieces but what can a fellow like himself do about it? Become giant-minded and build a new civilization—*him?* He says he's sorry but he has other engagements. He is due to play croquet with his aunt at twelve thirty.

One of the symptoms of indifference is boredom. I am appalled at the extent of boredom I see among Americans. It is especially tragic in the ranks of the younger people. They express it with the assumed sophistication of rebels (but they are not really rebellious), with a refusal to care. "Stay cool, man!" A famous movie of the 1960's, *Blow Up,* affords a fascinating commentary. It has to do with photography and a photographer, which is significant because that medium implies a separation of self from the thing photographed, with the picture taker involved in the plate and equipment but standing apart from the line subjects.

The movie dramatizes boredom in scene after scene. The photographer brings a group of models together in a studio; the models dress garishly and their faces are inhuman. In the middle of his picture taking the photographer walks outside, gets in his car, and drives away, leaving the models standing. He doesn't even tell them he is leaving, so little does he care about them. He goes into a lunchroom, finds a friend, and sits down to lunch. But after the waitress takes his order, he gets up and leaves without notice or explanation to either the friend or the waitress.

In the course of his photography he comes upon a murder. The crime is apparent from a photo he has taken. He returns to the place where he took the pictures and finds a dead body. But the murder is of no more importance to him than were the models or the waitress or the friend. He tells some friends whom he meets at a drug party about the murder but they pay no attention whatsoever. Indifference is still the prevailing order of the day. He goes back to see if the body is gone—it is, but that does not make much difference either. In the celebrated sex scene of the movie, he engages in a romp with two girls who come in to apply for jobs as models, but even in the midst of this frolic there is little emotion and when it is over he goes on with his work while the girls stand idly by, finally leaving in boredom.

One memorable scene involves a busload of clowns. They wave banners, blow horns, and throw streamers while the bus careens noiselessly around the streets. It appears to be a joyful and exciting event, but there is no sound, the streets are empty, and no one even watches. Who cares? Mirthless clowns, no fun, no involvement. The bus is driven to an empty park (the parks are always empty). Two of the clowns get out to play tennis, while the rest stand around watching. But the only sound is that of the tennis ball. In fact, there are no rackets and no ball, and when the ball is heard to bounce over the fence the clowns turn to watch, but there is nothing to watch. What is the difference?

This grim documentary about the emptiness, coldness, and detachment of people living within themselves is a portrayal of death, for part of the death wish is to get away from life. This is the extreme of "playing it cool." What is there to get excited about?

Of course there are other signs and symptoms of widespread indifference. Violence is one. The kinds of acts described in Chapter 7 are the last struggle of people saying, "Dammit, this life has got to have a point. If I have to destroy, I'll make it mean something!" If there is nothing to revere in qualitative growth, why not get rid of it? We feel enraged over a kind of betrayal—the promises of the spirit and of a full, rich life are empty and meaningless, a mockery.

But worse than violence itself, in my opinion, are our attitudes toward violence. It does not arouse us! We actually watch bombing raids on Vietnamese villages and hear about a lieutenant shooting down old people and children in cold blood, and we are not greatly

affected. Most of us wanted to protect Calley and explain his actions. Any year now I expect that we will
be sitting before our television sets and watching people in underdeveloped countries starve to death. Will
we feel deeply concerned? Riding shotgun in helicop-
ters, we hunt down deer, cougars, pumas, alligators,
leopards, kangaroos—not for food but for the sport of
it. Is this a sign of a people who care? Compare the
beautiful story of Jonah wherein God said he had to
protect the city even for the sake of the animals in it.
Then there is the corruption in our cities, which we
seem to tolerate so easily. There is organized crime—
again and again we are told by expert observers that it
flourishes partly because law-abiding, upright businessmen and others play along with it. In so many such
ways we exhibit overwhelming indifference. As Willie
Loman's wife cries in Miller's play, *"attention must be
paid."*

What are the causes of indifference? It is not due to
wanton maliciousness or some simple obvious factor.
Like the other sins described, indifference is not an
attitude to be pinned or blamed on someone. Indifference is part of us, bred into us—we cannot rid ourselves
of it. We can only seek to understand it for what it is
and, through our understanding, reduce it a little.

Surely one cause of present-day indifference is size
and complexity. In communities and nations so large
and complicated and difficult to control, how important can we be? We ask, "Could I affect the leadership
of our cities or improve social conditions enough to
reduce the amount of crime even if I tried?" Another
cause must be the effect of scientific attitudes. As
Nietzsche pointed out, science depends for its success
on impersonalness—we don't allow our preferences
and biases to affect the outcome of scientific experiments. This emphasis creates a tendency to regard

people and animals as things to be moved and manipulated. We begin acting like the machines and processes that we build. Still another cause is materialism. We emphasize money, position, power, and comfort so much that we wash out the emotions of the heart.

What, then, can we do about this deadly sin? I believe that the solution is for those of us who love life to "out-care" the drifters, stand-offers, and destroyers. We can care so much that we overcome their influence and reverse the horrible tendency. For this purpose we need brotherhoods of people who care. Men and women whose concern for life is greater than their desires to escape are everywhere in the world. We can find one another—if we try. We can come together for support, to preserve our sanity, to keep our hopes alive. We can do this in our families, in civic groups, in lodges, and surely best of all in our churches.

As an illustration, let me mention some of the ventures and activities undertaken by the congregation at Fountain Street Church in Grand Rapids, Michigan. Social action is not the purpose of our church; rather, we consider social action a by-product of caring and concern. But this partial list will serve as an example of what mutually supporting people can do. The congregation has been responsible for starting, organizing, and/or seeing through:

Reorganization of the juvenile court (separation of child dependents from the delinquent)

The beginnings of countywide cooperation in government

The Planned Parenthood Association

A chapter of the American Civil Liberties Union

The now well known Community Action Program

The West Michigan Environmental Action Association

Project Rehab (for dealing with the drug problem)

A consortium of local colleges

A police-community relations program (one of the first, if not the first, in the nation)

Establishment of group therapy as a common practice in social agencies and in the community

An abortion clinic

I must emphasize that running such projects is not considered to be the business of the church, though individuals in the congregation may stay involved with them after operations begin.

How would you like to feel that it would not matter to anyone if you died in the middle of the night, or that if you got sick, no one except your immediate family would care? This is the ultimate of indifference—the loss of individuality, the end of love.

The only way that we can handle the problems of size, complexity, scientific impersonality, and materialism is to *feel more.* It is by caring, feeling concern, and being involved that we find enough power to stop the barbarians who work only for a more efficient mechanical society. The possibility of such a "brave new world" is not remote. The signs and symbols of it are everywhere. To resist its advent, we must be willing to care, to be hurt, and to go on caring.

The Book of Jeremiah describes a man who wished to God that he could not feel anything anymore. He cursed and lamented the day he was born and given a heart, mind, and spirit. He cried out to God because of the pain, turmoil, unhappiness, and anxiety he experienced. He vowed he would no longer become involved or let himself become concerned. But then he found that he couldn't really turn away or stop caring. Jeremiah discovered that he couldn't release the burdens of his humanity.

The story reminds me of the cry of the primitive savage in Aldous Huxley's *Brave New World*.[32] In the end the savage cries out that he does not want to be peaceful. He wants to suffer. He wants God.

CHAPTER 10

Idolatry

Idolatry is perhaps the most difficult of the deadly sins to analyze. It is more subtle and abstract than the others. It is difficult to get people to pay attention, for the term seems so old-fashioned and the sin, if sin it be, so archaic. It is a sophisticated sin that only theologians and philosophers have paid much attention to. Yet this sin may well be the most important from a spiritual standpoint, even today.

Our understanding of the sin of idolatry comes from the Jews. It was the first sin they talked about. It ranked with murder. For example, when Moses came down from the mountaintop bringing the commandments of the Lord written on stones, he found his people worshiping a golden calf. They missed their old forms of reassurance, and without his binding, supportive presence they reverted to earlier and older comforts. Primitive and even later people have always deified objects in their environment or sanctified the animals on which they were dependent for survival. What was more important than a cow? It was and has been a sacred object for many millions, including the Hindus today. Survival and God are one and the same. When we worship the source of life, we worship God.

But, as we know from the Bible, Moses was wrathful with his people and excoriated them for falling away from the only true God. The commandments stated that the Lord was the God of all and there must be no other gods before him; no images or likenesses must be made of anything in the heavens, the earth, or the waters underneath the earth; and so there was to be no worship of images. In short, there must be nothing between the people and God. Any deity that could be represented was not the real God, for God is beyond representation. God lies behind all creation and must not be reduced or restricted to some thing or place however precious and important or revered.

This is a remarkable insight from such an early people. Through the centuries since Moses' time the Jews have strictly excluded any and all images or representations of deity. Modern religious sects have done the same, but the impetus and ideal come to us through the Jews. The genius of insight was theirs.

In itself an image is not idolatrous. It is only an aid to worship. For example, those who put pictures of the Virgin Mary behind candles and bow to that image are not actually worshiping the image—they know it is not the reality. It is only a call to remembrance, an effective way of focusing interest and attention. Images have served such purposes admirably from the beginnings of our humanity.

Idolatry takes place when we substitute the picture, icon, crucifix, or ideal for God himself. Anything can become holy and show forth the glory of God, including the simplest bush growing in the desert. But that bush or other image is not God, and if we let it come between us and God, we commit idolatry. So idolatry can be defined as the substitution of anything limited —from a golden calf to a church or a belief—for the unlimited. In the late Paul Tillich's terms, it is the substitution of the conditioned for the unconditioned. For the Jews, God was unconditioned because he was above all, beyond all, and in and through all. A conditioned thing may speak of God and for God but cannot be God. To put the thought in another way, idolatry is the substitution of something created for that which is the creator.

Idolatry is widespread because it is easy, manageable, satisfying, and tangible. Our own works and achievements are exalted into the divine. Thus we overcome our fear of dependence. When we make something controllable into God, God becomes our possession and is no longer the awe-inspiring creature mover. Idolatry appeals to our arrogance. We like to feel ourselves in control of life. Wasn't it given to us to manage and direct? When an idol is God, we eliminate the outside judge of our behavior—we ourselves become the judge—and no longer do we feel adrift in the infinite creativity of the universe.

Why is idolatry a spiritual sin and possibly the worst one? When we say that our best achievement is the reflection of God, we can justify stopping with that achievement. Thus it becomes not a window into God but an object beyond which we think we do not need to go. To illustrate, let us look at a series of short examples from history. The first six come from the Judeo-Christian experience and apply mostly to Western nations; the last two are universal in application.

First, the Jewish people fell into idolatry when they made their nation the ultimate of God's concern. Although rejecting tangible images, they fell into a more subtle trap. Seeing themselves as the chosen people, they found it easy to assume that God moved only

through them. They were to be the vehicle of God's
ascendancy in the world. This is why some of the Jewish prophets took it as their mission to attack their own
people, warning that they were mistaken in thinking
they were the chosen. The Jews might be the chosen
temporarily, the prophets warned, but if they did not
transcend themselves, God would choose another people in order to express his unlimited will in the life of
man.

In more recent times other nations have been in
desperate need of such prophecy. For decades the British crown—or perhaps the empire—was a symbol of
the ultimate for many Englishmen; near the end of his
famous lament in Shakespeare's *King Henry VIII,*
Cardinal Wolsey cries: "O Cromwell, Cromwell! Had I
but serv'd my God with half the zeal I serv'd my king."
Several decades ago, the swastika took the place of God
for many Germans under Hitler; the Aryans were the
chosen people and whatever they wanted was good for
all mankind, even if it meant destroying non-Aryans.
For the Soviet Union and the People's Republic of
China, communist ideology has been the ultimate.
Americans, too, have been guilty. One symptom is the
fear that many people have of criticizing our country.
If we did not make our country an "ultimate" or a
"necessity," there would be more freedom to transcend
our collective selves. "My country, right or wrong, but
my country" may not be so popular a motto now as it
used to be but it still has strong appeal.

Second, Jesus apparently exalted his role, at least,
for a while. We are not sure what he wanted and what
he dreamed for himself, but some of the record suggests that he may really have believed that God would
appear in person or that he himself was the divinely
anointed agent of God for the establishment of the
Kingdom. It seems certain he felt that something

unusual was destined for him, and believed that God was going to use him in some great and significant way. When he found that things were not going to work out in accordance with his expectations, his first reaction seemed to be: "I don't want it this way if I can avoid it. Let me be released from this." And then, near the end, he turned around in his thinking. Not his way but God's would prevail. He showed himself capable of subjecting his own divine sense of mission to the will of something higher. This act of self-correction may well be the supreme revelation of how God can break through our idolatry.

Third, the disciples of Jesus idolized him. They exalted their hopes for him to the point that he and their hopes took the place of God. When Jesus failed to meet their expectations and was crucified they deserted him. This, of course, was not the end of the deification of Jesus. From the beginning to our own day he has been idolatrized as God. The same thing happened to the Buddha despite his awareness of the possibility and his heroic effort to prevent it.

The cardinal weakness of Christianity—which, understandably, has been its greatest strength—is the making of Jesus into God. I have mentioned that Jesus sometimes seemed to think of himself as God but at other times he seemed to realize that he was just another person and that those who came after him would exceed his understanding and his achievements. I like to think of the cross as symbolizing the defeat of idols; it stands for the idea that the ideals we cherish most may obstruct the creative flow of fresh insight and understanding—of the goodness of God. The cross ended the hopes of a particular group of men—the finest and best men there were. But it did not end the hopes of mankind for new understanding.

Fourth, in the Middle Ages the Holy Catholic

Church assumed the role of spokesman for God. Its word was God's word; its promises were God's promises. Helpful and inspiring as this may have been, it nevertheless was frustrating and restrictive in the end. No wonder the Holy Catholic Church had so many quarrels with kings and emperors—the latter arrogated the same powers to themselves! Since the Middle Ages other Christian churches, using other divine techniques, have made themselves into the final word of God.

Fifth, Christians made the Bible an idol. They treated its statements as the last word—its word was the word of God. This kind of idolatry continues to this day among even the sophisticated. The fallacy is the same in principle as for the earlier examples. No matter how much insight the Bible may reveal, and however much God shines through it, it is the word and work of man. If God is the source of life and creativity, no person's or people's understanding can be the last word, for he is continually creating new life and working through fresh minds.

Sixth, Protestants have treated their beliefs and practices idolatrously. One church after another has said, "This is the way" or, "Our beliefs are right." As histories show, the result of this idolatry has been bitterness, resentment, cruelty, oppression, and wars that have destroyed hundreds of thousands of people. These dreadful results would not have happened if the churches had regarded their beliefs and practices as only their best human efforts whose function eventually was to give way to better beliefs and practices. The Protestant churches have not been tolerant or appreciative of the infinite diversity and possibilities of the human mind.

Seventh, we have idolized reason, science, and technocracy in the past century. Our implicit assumption has been that we could build a civilization so efficient and affluent that a transcendent being or power would not be necessary anymore. As we are only now becoming aware, this idolatry has been costly; it has shut off much of the creativity of God, by which I mean the creativity and growth that we might have experienced if we had realized how dependent we were on forces vaster and greater than any rational method or technological achievement. Friedrich Nietzsche was perhaps the first prophet to warn us of the dangers of this idolatry, but of course there have been many others since his time. However great our scientific advances, there is still a universe that man did not create; there is still the transformative power of God governing and directing in that universe. Not until we put aside our idolatrous devotion to our mechanical techniques and achievements can we hope to understand and appreciate some of the mysteries of that creative power.

Eighth, we have worshiped our virtues, strengths, and achievements. For many of us the golden calf has been fame, popularity, wealth, economic power, scholarship, truth, success, or even hard work. We may be too sophisticated to admit that these represent God for us, but our actions belie us. We push ourselves to the limit to get more publicity, more friends, more controls. We lack the faith to let ourselves be led beyond our chosen, familiar, comfortable standards and procedures. Jesus let God lead him to the cross; that is to say, he had faith enough to see the possibilities in ways that were other than he had chosen, other than what he liked or found pleasing. This is in large part the meaning of the cross. It is a revelation of the peculiar, open, adventurous nature of the religious way.

The Selfishness of Idealism

One reason why idolatry is so dangerous and destructive is that it goes under socially approved names, such as patriotism, public service, and good work. For example, patriotic devotion can be as selfish as individual self-aggrandizement. It can be, and often is, a cover-up for acquisitiveness—we do for our country what we would find unworthy to do for ourselves. Some will recall the famous statement by the Italian statesman Mazzini: "If we had done for ourselves the things that we have done for our country, what scoundrels we would be." Of course, not all patriots are scoundrels; my point is only that this form of idealism is a frequent escape hatch for selfish people. The same goes for such ideals as justice, racial equality, and equal opportunity. How often we find that workers for such causes take leave, in the name of their cause, to corrupt or destroy or lay up much wealth and power for themselves. Some of the worst tyrants in the world boast of their lack of greed for wealth or of their sexual purity or their love for children or mother, but they have no qualms whatsoever in imposing the worst of tortures on their enemies or stealing the world's finest art or destroying the world's most beautiful cities.

Almost invariably there is some pride in every form of idealism. We can display power and have people respect us for it where they would not respect gluttony or acquisitiveness. For many religious thinkers, power and pride are among the worst of sins because they are so close to the "throne of God" and can be talked about in such idealistic terms.

One of the most widely respected and knowledgeable men in the investigation of the Watergate scandals was Archibald Cox. He cites four cases as evidence of the moral decline that led to the much-publicized break-in at the Democratic headquarters. Notice how power and idealism figure in Cox's description of the cases:

> For the first case, choose one of the more aggressive tactics by confrontation pursued by student activists during the wave of unrest in 1968–1971: the physical seizure of buildings, the bombing of the laboratory at the University of Wisconsin or of Harvard's Center for International Affairs Library, the burning of R.O.T.C. buildings, and the disruption of public meetings so that views distasteful to the activists were denied expression. Many participants in these activities were sincerely convinced of the righteousness of their objectives. . . .
>
> Case two is the Berrigans and the destruction of Selective Service records. The sincerity of their belief is generally acknowledged.
>
> Daniel Ellsberg provides the third example. Dr. Ellsberg's motives appear to have been highly moral. He doubtless thought that he was performing a great service to both his country and to humanity . . . when he "stole" the Pentagon Papers.
>
> The fourth case is that of Egil Krogh, the head of the "White House plumbers." . . . Krogh, from everything I have learned, sincerely believes himself to be, and in that sense is, a highly moral man. At the time he approved the violation of Dr. Fielding's and Daniel Ellsberg's civil rights he sincerely viewed the action as a service to his country and humanity.
>
> Does an important common thread run through these four cases? There is a wealth of distinctions ranging from trivialities to substantial differences in both conduct and justification, yet I doubt the distinctions are critical. . . . In each case, the actor believed his wrong to be justified by the righteousness of his cause and the need for drastic means to achieve his objective.[33]

What causes extremism, fanaticism, and some of the other expressions of idolatry? One cause is fear—fear of the loss of a favorite idea, belief, way, type of security, position, or other cherished thing. All people have such fears but the extremist has them stronger than most of us do.

Anxiety is another cause. The extremist has great fear, but he is not sure exactly what he is afraid of. His fear is diffused, vague, and nonspecifiable. Senator Joseph McCarthy in the 1950's was a classic example.

Inability to stand the tension of differences is also characteristic of extremists. As long as things are not final, firm, solid, and "right," he or she feels a desperate need to end the uncertainty, a terrible impatience with efforts to proceed through understanding. "Let's get the answer. Let's get it fast, and forget the cost!"

Long before the splurge of concern over extremism in the 1960's, the late Paul Tillich observed that the fanatic is one who in the effort to resolve his (or her) doubts has had to destroy his freedom. I find that to be a beautiful expression of the problem. The fanatic is necessarily subject to the pulls and tensions that trouble all people. But in order to find peace of mind, he must latch onto something sure and hard, and then assert himself over others in order to compensate for the doubting self he wants to hide. But the more he tries to subject that latter part of himself, the louder it shouts to be heard, and so the more necessary it becomes to attack the selfhood of others. The fanatic is forever attacking, forever screaming in self-assertion while trying desperately to prevent himself from committing suicide.

Although the effects of extremism and fanaticism are more drastic than are the effects of other forms of idolatry, I want to enumerate them because they dramatize the evils of idolatrous worship in whatever guise it is found:

1. *Spiritual hell.* For the fanatic, there is no peace of mind or feeling of sharing and belonging to the immense, mysterious, infinite creativity of life, viz., God. Compulsions to attack others, intolerable insecurity, neurotic doubting—these and other symptoms indicate the horrors commonly endured by this type of sinner no matter how great his or her success in the power struggle.

2. *Loss of freedom.* From the early Christian zealots to the "law and order" totalitarians of today, fanatics have not allowed freedom for others in the areas where they have operated. For both personal and ideological reasons, they cannot brook differences of opinion on fundamentals. Even in their writings, if they produce any, fanatics indicate the need to curtail freedom for the sake of long-range goals.

3. *Loss of dignity.* How can another person walk in dignity when he or she must bow to the fanatic? Behavior is dictated, personal expression is subjected to higher approval, privacy is invaded.

4. *Fear and terror.* Terrorist methods are used against those who do or may disagree. Speakers are shouted down. Justice is perverted. The "Manual" was the Nazi approach in the 1930's and 1940's, but we see the extremist's tactics all over the world today, perhaps not as open and organized as in Hitler's regime but continually threatening.

Thus, fanaticism and extremism victimize both subject and object. Fanatics have never contributed anything to freedom. Even when they oppose something that is inadequate or undesirable (such as irresponsible students or a wayward press), they succeed only in substituting behavior that is worse. We must find the strength to tolerate the fanatics, but we must not let them take over.

The United States was formed in an enlightened day by men of reason who rarely claimed absolutist positions. Much the same could be said of many other nations in the world. The founders of this country did not deceive themselves into thinking that they had the final answers. They were willing to listen, and they did listen, to others. They knew there was no position that could not be defended *or* attacked. They knew that different times, needs, and circumstances lay ahead, and they wrote a constitution that took this important fact into consideration. Our Constitution is the product of numerous compromises made by men who believed ardently in certain causes and methods but who recognized that they could be wrong and were wonderfully willing to entertain ideas they did not like. This maturity of belief is written into the Constitution, is guaranteed by it, and is one reason for its creative influence and durability.

In conclusion, let us remember that anything can become holy, anything can reveal God. But there is nothing that should be put in the place of God. We must realize the limitations of our best and strongest ideas, approaches, people, and achievements. In religious terms, we must hear the word of God spoken against our sins. In a creative, pulsing, changing, dynamic world of process, perhaps nothing is more important than this quality of self-awareness and finiteness. Perhaps no sin is worse than that of making our achievements, desires, practices, and beliefs some sort of ultimate ideal.

Those things should be sacred and holy which are a source of inspiration, guidance, and strength for us. In this sense the Bible is sacred and holy, for the simple but persuasive reason that it speaks continually to the heart and mind, and we ignore numerous of its insights at our own risk and the possibility of our destruction. One such passage is contained in the writings of the prophet Micah:

> "With what shall I come before the LORD,
>   and bow myself before God on high?
> Shall I come before him with burnt offerings,
>   with calves a year old?
> Will the Lord be pleased with thousands of rams,
>   with ten thousands of rivers of oil?
> Shall I give my first-born for my transgression,
>   the fruit of my body for the sin of my soul?"
> He has showed you, O man, what is good;
>   and what does the LORD require of you
> but to do justice, and to love kindness,
>   and to walk humbly with your God?
>
> (Micah 6:6–8)

Part III

SALVATION IS
LOVE OF LIFE

CHAPTER 11

What It Takes to Be Saved

If we are all sinners, and if we are fated by nature and circumstance to do evil, even as we do good, then we should all be interested in salvation. The word "salvation" appears frequently in writing and discussion, so much so that we are inclined to regard it as a peculiarly Christian term, lacking in meaning outside the Christian community. Members of other religions talk about the "illumined," the "enlightened," people who are "fulfilled," "awareness," "children of light," and the "awakened ones." They do not talk about salvation.

In Christian usage, salvation often means that a person is rescued from fatal, deadly sin to a life of eternal bliss. A person is either saved or not saved. Salvation is clear, obvious, final, irreversible, and unmistakable. There are no shades of gray of salvation—you have it or you do not.

The theory of this venerable Christian concept follows this line of reasoning: God created a perfect world and put a perfect man in it, but this man disobeyed God and fell into a state of imperfection and sin. From that

time forth, according to the Scriptures, man was
doomed to wander in darkness, with no means of his
own to regain his original state. But God sent his son,
Jesus, to earth and let him be sacrificed in order to
provide man with an opportunity to redeem himself.
Note that the opportunity was given by God; it was not
and could not be earned by man. This was logical.
Since the fall of man was transcendental, his salvation
had to be transcendental. But all man had to do was say
"I believe" and he could be saved. It did not matter
where and how he did this—in joy, in pain, in war or
peace, in jail or in a foxhole or in church. He would be
saved from damnation if he acknowledged that God
came in the person of Jesus to reconcile himself to
mankind.

According to this orthodox view, those who are
saved know it. They gain a remarkable sense of assurance and joy. They are released from all pain of the
spirit (though not physical pain), from all doubt, from
all worry and anxiety. They become sure of their destiny. Their world is transformed.

For nearly twenty centuries this orthodox version of
salvation endured and was meaningful to most of
Western civilization. Today it strikes a large and rapidly growing number of people as a myth—beautiful
and insightful but an unsatisfactory explanation of
reality. It is inconsistent with our expanding knowledge of the nature of the universe. It is at odds with our
scientific as well as our workaday knowledge of ourselves. What is more, the proclaimed effects of supernatural salvation on saved people seem open to some
obvious questions. When we observe the "saved," we do
not always find assurance, joy, peace, and confidence
in their behavior. Nor are these qualities, when we
find them in such a person, traceable only to the claim
of salvation; often they seem to be due more to family

training and general environment. Moreover, these same qualities may be found equally as often, if not more frequently, among people who reject this notion of supernatural salvation. There is also the important question, discussed earlier in this book, of whether unquestioning, undoubting sureness is really a good quality. As noted in earlier chapters, absolute conviction can be destructive—the history of Christianity itself is full of such evidence. What is more, often in personal experience we find that growth in understanding and maturity comes *because of* doubt, anxiety, and pain. The spirit does not thrive on certainty and joy alone.

I suggest that there are other ways of looking at salvation than through the eyes of this orthodox, traditional conception. I shall describe one such way here. I do not hold it up as *the* way, and as man gains more knowledge and perspective in the future, this way too will need to be revised. But I believe that it is valid in terms of what we know now about man and the world —it can be tested and discussed objectively. And it has, in my experience, proved to be a helpful, realistic guide for many people. It is flexible, and it makes sense.

Salvation is a knowledge, a feeling, an awareness, or an appreciation of God. When a person finds that which in his or her estimation is utterly necessary to all life, and develops a sense of belonging to or participating in that reality, then an element of salvation is present. One's existence is not then a casual or accidental event—here today and gone tomorrow. There is a felt creative, sustaining, inspiring relationship with the whole world, with all that has happened before, with all that shall ever happen in the future.

Salvation must be an aspect of the individual's own knowledge and appreciation, not someone else's. We may draw on the knowledge and insight of others, but we must put it together in our own way. As this implies, salvation is not a transcendental transaction of some sort, as in conventional Christianity. It is a person's natural relationship with the natural environment. Therefore it does not depend upon a particular kind of confession, types or frequency of prayer, or the doing of acts in ways specified by authorities or institutions.

Salvation is both an achievement and a gift. It is an achievement because a person has to work for insight and knowledge. Questioning, doubting, supposing, testing, perhaps arguing—all these are part of the process. But salvation is also a legacy. For if there is some magnificent creative force behind us all, we are created creatures with the capacity for salvation bred into us. Though this capacity is not given to us in equal amounts, it can be developed by anyone who wants to apply diligence, discipline, and training.

It follows that man is responsible for his own salvation. The need to be saved is his problem. His dividedness between conscious and subconscious, between himself and his fellowman, and between himself and nature is a predicament he has to wrestle with. No paternal power is going to bail him out.

It follows also that salvation is never complete, never finished. If God and creativity are a process, so must salvation be. We see God through a glass darkly. We can clean the glass and learn to see better through it, but our eyes and understanding are finite—though the limits of finiteness can be rolled back.

Not only is the process never complete, but the saved person may not even know that he (or she) is saved. He may feel such a strong sense of belonging to the creative source of all being, as he perceives it, that he makes no division between himself and that source; he does not say: "Behold how wonderful I am. Look where I have been and where I am going." In this respect, too, salvation in the new sense is different from the orthodox interpretation, where the saved person is sure of his good fortune.

What are the characteristics of people who are finding salvation in the modern sense? To put the question in another way, what tendencies and qualities become stronger in those persons who identify with the source of their being? My observation suggests the following:

First, their sensitivity grows. As they relate themselves to God, they grow more aware of the countless interdependencies about them and, seeing these connections, respond to them more appreciatively. This process is the opposite of hatred and indifference, which are marked by increasing insensitivity and rejection of the ties that bind and relate.

Second, they become more flexible. Recognizing that there is a force greater than themselves, they understand that no matter how wondrous they and their institutions are, their achievement is far from the ultimate; no matter how right their answers seem to be in relation to what other people are saying, those answers are not final. Therefore they are more alert to possibilities they would not dream of otherwise. Hamlet had the idea: "There are more things in heaven and earth, Horatio, Than are dreamt of in your philosophy."

Third, their humility grows. It could hardly be otherwise, for they see themselves, with their limitations of an animal heritage, in relation to the boundless creativity of God. The book *Papillon* has been a best seller because it reports the sensational escapes of its author from French prisons. But it also documents this remarkable man's efforts to understand God. One of Papi's revelations came during his escape on a small

raft from Devil's Island, and he describes how humble
he felt:

> The tears in my pus-filled eyes became a thousand little
> crystals of every color. Like stained-glass windows, I
> thought. God is with you today, Papi! In the midst of na-
> ture's monstrous elements, in the wind, the immenseness
> of the sea, the depth of the waves, the imposing green roof
> of the bush, you feel your own infinitesimal smallness,
> and perhaps it's here, without looking for Him, that you
> find God, that you touch Him with your finger. I had
> sensed Him at night during the thousands of hours I had
> spent buried alive in dank dungeons without a ray of sun;
> I touched Him today in a sun that would devour every-
> thing too weak to resist it. I touched God, I felt Him around
> me, inside me. He even whispered in my ear: "You suffer;
> you will suffer more."[34]

Fourth, people who are finding salvation as I define
it become marked by the quality of forgiveness. They
become more knowing about their imperfections and
sinfulness; they make fewer pretensions to innocence
and perfection in their relationships with other people. Just as they are hurt by others, they realize that
they also inflict harm on loved ones and friends. They
know they need to be received back by those whom
they have hurt.

Fifth, their tenderness, reverence, and devotion become more marked. To seek more understanding of
God is to grow in awareness of goodness, love, beauty,
and other conditions on which an individual is dependent. As such awareness grows, one deals more rever-
ently with people and gains respect for what they are
trying to do. "I'm passionately involved in life," pianist
Artur Rubinstein once remarked. "I love its change, its
color, its movement. To be alive, to be able to see, to
walk, to have houses, music, paintings—it's all a miracle."

Sixth, finding salvation produces strength. The qualities of humility and tenderness just mentioned do not mean any loss in resilience, drive, or desire to succeed. The people I am describing sometimes acquire prodigious strength because of their sense of belonging to an eternal, universal process of creativity from which they cannot be cut off. Their day is not the only day of that process, and if their hopes for fulfillment are not realized now, they will be tomorrow. "If not in my life, then in another life."

Seventh, the people I am describing have faith and hope. The horrors in the world do not blind them to the ubiquitous presence of a life-force working in an incredible variety of ways—a force that was here before them and that will continue long after them, carrying man to unimagined heights of achievement.

Eighth, people who are finding salvation give of themselves. Whether they are wealthy or poor, their lives are marked by measures of service and sacrifice. Feeling related to that great and mysterious process of evolution, they reach out to help—it is not altruism. They serve the present, which they know, and they also serve the future, which they do not know. The words of an unknown African chief, as reported by early European colonists, convey this sense of stewardship:

> This land belongs to my people.
> Some of them are dead.
> Some of them are living.
> But most of them have not yet been born.[35]

Ninth, the state of salvation is characterized by growth in cognitive understanding. People who are finding God never find God completely. The more they sense and learn of him, the greater their stimulus to

reach out for more understanding. This need to grow
has been expressed in almost countless ways by people
who are great in spirit. Here is the way Albert Einstein
stated the need in a letter to a rabbi who had written
for counsel:

> A human being is a part of the whole, called by us "Uni-
> verse," a part limited in time and space. He experiences
> himself, his thoughts and feelings as something separated
> from the rest—a kind of optical delusion of his conscious-
> ness. This delusion is a kind of prison for us, restricting us
> to our personal desires and to affection for a few persons
> nearest to us. Our task must be to free ourselves from this
> prison by widening our circle of compassion to embrace
> all living creatures and the whole nature in its beauty.
> Nobody is able to achieve this completely, but the striving
> for such achievement is in itself a part of the liberation
> and a foundation for inner security.[36]

Eternal Life

It took aeons for man's self-consciousness to evolve.
This precious capacity which introduced him to God
and allowed him to see himself as part of God was
something he did not want to let go. Ever since the
dawn of human consciousness, man has been trying to
hold on to his selfhood. He hates to relinquish it. His
fight against death is the ultimate of his struggle
against the many restrictions and limitations on consciousness. Seeking to be like God and to have eternal
life, he has failed in the biophysical sense but suc-
ceeded in the metaphysical sense. He devised a number of philosophies that would assure him of eternal
life.

The first such device was the belief that his physical
body would continue after death—that what appeared
to be the end of life was not that really. This primitive

notion still survives in some cultures, but of course it has long since been abandoned in most areas of the world.

Then came the concept of the soul or spirit as an entity within the body but separate from it. When the body died, the soul was released so it could exist in another realm, such as heaven or an astral body. Orthodox Christianity, the Church of the Latter-day Saints, theosophy, and other faiths have held to this concept.

The third approach to maintaining selfhood is Eastern—reincarnation, or the law of Karma. It is believed that after physical death the self reincorporates from time to time until the Karma is exhausted. At that point the self ceases to be an individual soul and merges with the infinite soul; it goes back to the great sea of being called God.

Both the Christian and Eastern philosophies recognize that death is the loss of selfhood. But in their contrasting ways they see that death is not the end, that it leads to the discovery of a greater self, an eternal being. Whether this greater being is called God consciousness, cosmic consciousness, superconsciousness, or something else is irrelevant; the important thing is the insight that with death the barriers of individuality are overcome and being becomes more than temporal. We find our peace in that from which we emerged, for we were here before birth in the stuff of the universe. Life as a human being is a particular form of consciousness, a particular form of God. Death means going back to the greater consciousness, the eternal creative force.

Kazantzakis has expressed this idea beautifully.[37] He says that we are not the tree but leaves on the tree. As leaves we summarize and symbolize the vitality of the tree. Everything that happens in the tree happens in us. We feel every movement in the roots, the trunk, the branches. The metaphor is helpful and necessary, because of course we have no objective experience to bring to bear on life after death. We are not now discussing an objective reality. We are referring only to hopes, ideas, or feelings that we use to give our life more dignity, meaning, strength, and purpose. This natural and venerable desire is best served through metaphor.

Other analogies are possible. For instance, we might say that our lives are not the face of God but expressions on the face. As expressions come and go, the face remains, forever giving rise to new expressions. Though the expressions are fleeting, they *are* the face. Still another analogy is sparks of a fire. A spark is a momentary expression of a fire; when the spark dies, the fire is there to continue throwing off sparks. In the same way, an individual is an expression of God. The creative power that gave him or her life continues after the body returns to dust. Does the fire die because the spark goes out? Neither does the spirit die when the body is gone.

What is redemption? We are redeemed, I believe, when we rise above our self-involvement in business and pleasure to catch a glimpse of how we belong to life and how it creates and is created. Does it matter much what religious form we use to gain this understanding? I think not. The important point is that when we see that we belong, we have no further worry about our individual selfhoods. We are redeemed from alienation—that is, we know we are not apart from the universe, creation, and life's creativity, but part of them, of the same substance as they are. I interpret this to be the redemption which Jesus talked about; this is also the redemption Buddha described.

To grow in the recognition of who, what, and why we are is to be saved from futility, emptiness, nothingness. We do not have to wonder then about the significance of our little lives, for we see ourselves as part of the tree of eternal life. The tree works through us, it exists in us, and indeed it may well be said that we are God and that we save God (instead of vice versa) by doing his work on this planet. Such understanding saves us from self—from the greed, exploitativeness, and viciousness that would characterize us if we acted out of narrow self-interest alone. The story of the good Samaritan illustrates the function of unselfishness in the simplest terms, and that is why we have used the parable so long to teach our children. Its moral is that the way to acquire is to give. More broadly, the way to win life is to lose it. The way to find one's self is to see it as part of a larger self. The more a person tries to hold on to the spark, the less he or she has of the fire. Thus Jesus said that he and the Father were one; he did not seek redemption as an individual apart from God. He told his disciples they would do greater things than he had done. If he was the son of God, so were they.

This line of thought may help to explain repeated observations that I have made over the years as a counselor to numerous people. These observations are the basis of what I like to call a spiritual law. Like so many such laws, this one sounds paradoxical, and although it does not conform to everyone's experience, I find ever-increasing evidence to support it: The more a person loves life, the less he or she fears death. The more richly and abundantly (in a spiritual sense) the person has lived, the less concern he or she feels about mortality. The man or woman who has not tasted, who has not felt deeply, who has not loved well, who has not known, who has not participated, is the one who feels disturbed and anxious and fear-ridden about the prospect of dying.

It is almost impossible to conceive of a good, beautiful, human life that is not based on qualities like those described earlier in this chapter. They are the characteristics of a saved person. That is to say, they are the qualities of a person intimately and knowingly related to the mystery and vigor of natural life—call it God, if you will.

CHAPTER 12

How Much
Can We Do
with Willpower?

Authorities do not talk much about willpower any-more. Not for a long time have I heard someone eulo-gize it or even defend it. It is supposed to be an old-fashioned virtue in an age where motivation, incen-tives, psychological conditioning, and vitamins are what really count.

But there is much validity in the old-fashioned vir-tue of will, and it ought not to be lost in psychology. I have enormous respect for psychology—my under-standing of it is the source of numerous ideas to be presented—but I do not believe that we are justified in using it to exclude the factor of individual will. It does not seem to me that the identity we have characterized as willpower can be lost or diminished if our culture is to remain humane. It is urgent that we understand the potentials of the will if we are to take a construc-tive approach toward modern sins.

What is the will? It does not characterize animals. There may be some of it in a dog or a raccoon, but the amount is so little as to be unimportant. Will is coequal and coexistent with the definition of humanity, for it is only the human mind that discriminates and chooses, and only a choosing mind can be said to will anything. We can see conditions and varieties of conditions. We can weigh and evaluate those things which are most important to us. We can see that many things that we ought to do we will leave undone. We can understand why we do things we ought not to do. We know the difference between desire, pleasure, and obligation. We can distinguish between obligation and responsibility. In short, we can choose our way.

We can—but we don't. At least, that seems to be what many authorities are saying and thinking. In fact, anyone who suggests that we use willpower to solve our problems may be laughed at. If we have a problem, we take a drug (including alcohol, perhaps) to solve it. Or we resort to a psychological justification for our attitude and then find a drug so we can live with the consequences of that attitude. We take pills to help us sleep or wake up, gain or lose weight, raise or lower our energy levels, increase or decrease our sensitivity and awareness.

Do advances in psychology, medicine, biology, and other sciences mean that human nature is now radically altered so that we no longer should try to act as choosing, deciding men and women as our ancestors did? If we forfeit our ability to discriminate and choose, can we be said to be Homo sapiens still? We have willed that one day man will live on this planet without fear of war. Do we stop willing that, letting the outcome be determined instead by the interplay of events? We have willed that the future will be better for our children. Do we concede that question also to conditioning influences and environmental trends? Do we stop hoping?

I hear students say, "I don't like school." This may

be their excuse for, say, dropping out or seeking an escape through drugs. I answer: "What difference does it make whether you like it or not? Would that you like it, but don't you think you could will your way through it?" I hear people say they don't like their work, using that as an excuse for something destructive they do. I answer: "Would that you could have a job that you liked, but is there no element of will? Are you determined by the job or do you decide what the job is worth? Can you not place your job in perspective with other things you want and decide if the price of your job is worth paying—and if not, what alternative is worthwhile?"

Why should the things we want be pleasant? Whoever said they must be? Humanity was not made by pursuing the pleasant course but by tackling difficult problems so that there could be a better world. I wonder if there is any individual problem that a strong person cannot overcome with his or her will. For example, I hear it said that some people have sex drives that are too hard to handle—the compulsions are too deeply rooted in them. While I appreciate that sex drives are a severe problem for some people, that fact does not mean they are beyond the control of one's will. Or, consider the moods with which we start some days. We may move into an ugly or pessimistic mood as though it had precedence over our will. In my own case, the mood seems to grow sometimes as if it were something apart from me, apart from what I see and hear. For the world is the same. And I know from experience that if I will myself to look around with different eyes and listen with different ears, the mood will change. I can wash that mood away by taking action with mind and spirit.

This is not to say that I or anyone else can do all we want to do, or that there are not times when our bur-

dens become so great that we need help. We are all
limited, our burdens are unequal, our strengths vary
greatly. All this I recognize fully. I am writing in behalf of a neglected cause, the will, and my point is that
everyone has the capacity to make choices and move
in the directions of those choices. Though a person be
weak and disadvantaged, he or she can govern some of
the conditions of life, for always there are some conditions that can be changed by understanding.

Several years ago a beautiful movie, *Charly,* attracted much attention. It was the story of a dolt who
in the dimness of his mind had a desire to learn. He
also had a will to succeed, and this will drove him
night after night to try to learn how to read and write.
Charly's determination to do better and amount to
something touched many people, and for good reason:
Everyone has the potential to do better, and our failure
to use it more is due not to the reality of human nature
but to a quirk in our culture. Let me explain.

Willpower could not possibly be used to its fullest by
someone faithful to orthodox, traditional Christianity.
Take Paul's struggle as reported in the Bible. It was a
fight against himself. Paul's point was that man's
natural impulses and desires are wicked, and that the
only way he can be redeemed is to be re-created by
God. Man cannot transcend himself by the power of
his own will—he is too evil to be able to do that. So his
earthly existence is a struggle against himself—
against the desires of the flesh, as though the flesh
were evil. Orthodox Christianity still preaches this
doctrine, and it is believed by many millions of people.
Moreover, it is part of the Victorian approach and
puritanical tradition that continue to underlie so
much of our moral thinking.

The result is a morality that is unreal to us: To be
moral according to the dictates of the orthodox Chris-

tian church we must betray our human natures. To live up to standards that are antihuman, antipersonal, antifeeling, and antinatural, such as avoidance of the seven deadly sins of the Middle Ages, we must defeat ourselves as natural human beings because pride, envy, anger, and the rest are part of our makeup. And when self fights self, it is obvious that the only loser is self. But the self will not tolerate such a defeat. Sooner or later the defeated natural self will have its vengeance. Any victory over it in the name of will is precarious. The self that has lost its validity, authority, honor, and pride will fight to gain the upper hand. It will not allow willpower to keep winning.

If we are going to enhance the dignity of the individual, we must develop practices that reflect and glorify the individual rather than degrade, diminish, or reject him. This means using the magnificent power we call willpower in another way.

Often willpower is described as if it were a desire: Because I want something, I will rouse myself to achieve it. But willpower is far more than this. It has to be, because there are all kinds of diverse, inconsistent desires and wishes in an individual, all natural, all honorable. Hence we must find the courage to cut through the screen of feelings about our nature that religion and society have created. When we do that, we will find selves that are worthy of respect. We have destructive wishes and we do wicked things, but when we understand how we came to be this way we can rally our wills to transcend the evil desires. Not that we will achieve perfection—we will not. But we can grow in understanding and devotion, thus moving toward the achievement of a heavenly kingdom in this world.

Let's try a few illustrations. Suppose you want to stop smoking. Why? Because your doctor urged you to. Because medical science indicates that smoking is

dangerous to your health. You don't want to run the
risk. Here, therefore, is a simple desire. But other
desires conflict with it. You want the comfort and reassurance of that cigarette. You want the diversion it
offers. You want something in your hands between you
and a situation—it helps to still your nervousness. And
you enjoy the taste and smell of tobacco. So here you
have two sets of desires fighting each other. Both of
them are you. Both are honorable, human, understand-
able. What happens if you apply an enormous effort of
will to stop smoking? The desires for comfort, diversion, reassurance, and pleasure continue to work on
you, do they not? Therefore one day in a weak moment
—for willpower—that desire will win. But who wins
really? Nobody. Self has lost. Self always loses when
one part of it loses to another.

I will return to this dilemma shortly, but first let us
look at a few other illustrations. You want to stop
drinking. You know that alcohol is destroying your life;
you've seen the signs, though you may not admit it to
friends. On the other hand, you do not want to lose the
escape that alcohol gives you. You do not want to con-
front yourself. You do not want to remember Mama or
to recognize your need for her (the nipple, stroking,
and so forth). Now, you may exert your willpower
enough to stop drinking for a while. Sheer, disciplined
suppression of the "desires of the flesh" may be trium-
phant for weeks or months. But the trouble is that the
defeated desires are valid, too, and they will fight to
have their way. And one day you will take what is
called a careless or occasional drink, and the next
thing you know you will be drinking regularly again.

You want to lose weight. Then you will be more attractive, desirable, healthy. Perfectly valid desires. But
food brings you reassurance and boosts your ego in a
way that nothing else does. Those are legitimate, hon-

orable desires too. So when you determine to diet and your will wins, another part of you loses, a part that, unlike the lost weight, does not disappear. And that defeated part will not submit but will fight to have its way. And it will succeed, sooner or later.

You want to be rich and successful. Almost everyone has had this wish. But it is not an easy wish to carry out because it conflicts with yearnings for leisure and camaraderie; besides, striving for success means tension, the demands of power, and deprivation. You may indeed drive yourself to riches and power, but you can be sure the other side will never cease nagging. Willpower brings no victory for the self in this case either.

You want to be independent, to express your mind boldly and freely, to stand up against a member of your family, the boss, your church, or government. Here is a noble desire, celebrated all down through our history. *But* you do not like being unattractive to many people, do you? You do not like to create hard feelings and disharmony, do you? One set of desires comes at the expense of the other, and you cannot have them both.

Such examples make it clear that willpower has to be more than desire. It has to be a unity of self or it cannot hope to stay on top. When the self makes a choice as a *total* self, the decision can carry amazing strength—the strength, as people often say, to move mountains. How do we make choices in this way, that is, develop true willpower?

We must have values based on a knowledge of who we are—not on a knowledge of what society or the church says that we should be, but on facts, insights, and observations that in *our* estimation can stand up any time they are tested. Is your desire for comfort real? Is your desire to protect your ego real? What about your wish to be loved? To be master of your own fate? To be attractive and desirable? Any of these can be real and honorable desires—humanity could not have survived without them.

Therefore, if you want to stop smoking, the answer depends on your understanding of yourself. What I as a counselor urge you or your doctor warns you is beside the point. There is no "ought" from the outside that will do the trick. The question is: Do you as a self want to stop smoking? Can your health *and* your pleasure be satisfied if you stop? If you find that they can, after reflecting on your values, then willpower is on your side and you can succeed. You understand your wishes for health, comfort, and reassurance as one. You would be an idiot then if you did not agree to stop smoking. Of course you will miss the nice taste and feel of the cigarette, and you may dream about it for months, but your whole person is behind the commitment now— and that total self is not willingly or easily defeated. It is when you are a "house divided" that you do not have the willpower to succeed.

Much the same is true of the other problems mentioned. In every case the resolution is invalid if it implies self-defeat. Accordingly, I advise a person to stop running away from an escape if he or she really wants it. If you demand the ego satisfaction that food gives you, then stop fussing about your diet. If you're unwilling to live with the fact that you need Mama, stop trying to give up alcohol. You can't win a civil war with yourself. But at the same time, don't pretend that the ego satisfaction or fear of Mama is unimportant. If they are important, they are valid—no need to cover them up.

Nor do you have to kid yourself about the cost of achievement or of giving up a habit, if that is your choice. You don't need hypnosis or to repeat several times a day that you don't really like alcohol or the price of fame. There is a cost and it may be quite noticeable. But you are willing to pay it—not just willing, *eager*—because it is for a unified you.

One individual looks at another and thinks: "My, I'd like to be that strong and courageous. It must take fantastic strength." But the second, if he hears the thought, might reply: "It doesn't take much strength. I wouldn't buy the alternative—I couldn't afford it. This is what I want, this is me. I pay the cost gladly because I buy my pride and honor."

Willpower does not enable us to eliminate sinfulness, only to cope with it and manage it more effectively. Nor does it enable us to do away with evil, only to see it better and reduce it while we work to increase the good in our lives. In the long evolution of human life, willpower is a comparatively new resource, and it may be that we have only begun to tap its potentials.

CHAPTER 13

The Religious Answer

Sin is totally natural, completely inescapable, and therefore, I think, basically good. Although we want to check and control it, we cannot live without it. For sin has to do with the nature of man. We have been taught that when man sins, he betrays his humanity. This is not so. When he sins, he *expresses* his humanity, for to be human is to be an animal seeking to become God. Sin can exist only at the human level, because it belongs to a limited consciousness aware of its limitations and seeking to transcend them. The animal cannot sin, and God is perfection. Man is constantly reaching beyond the animal toward perfection. But as long as he is human he never can become perfect, nor can he ever be an animal again, no matter how low he sinks. Therefore he lives inescapably with sin.

We have been doubly taught on this matter. We are embarrassed and ashamed of our sinfulness, and we ought not to be. Our sin is our challenge, our promise, our special quality. It is that which confronts us when consciousness and self-knowledge lead us to place ourselves at the center of the universe, seeing everything in life as moving around us and having pertinence, relativity, and value only for us, as if nothing else counted. Sin is born out of our conscious self-centeredness in necessary conflict with our total dependence and interdependence. We see that we must come to terms with our neighbors, who stand in the same center point of reference but with the whole universe moving around them. The universe moves around each of us, yet we have to relate to one another.

Indeed, we find that we can be human only *as* we relate to one another. To do that, we have to come out of the self-enclosures of our individuality, out of this containment that is our self, with its own peculiar knowledge, awareness, and feelings. Nobody else can possibly know, no matter how carefully we lay it out or express it in words, deeds, song, or dance, just what constitutes our private world of feeling and awareness. Yet we have to relate to somebody else who is also a unique, self-contained, Godlike being. As long as we are human and do not transcend our human state, we will have to deal with this dynamic interrelatedness merely to stay alive. The quality of our humanity will depend on the degree and quality of our interrelationships.

Although we can never revert to preconscious animal life, the animal lives on in us. We are burdened and blessed by an ancestry of millions of years of unconscious animal existence. As we try to reach out, to be more than the elemental, to be more than simply living process, the animal drags us back. Hence, in times of confusion we may feel a great desire to lose conscious awareness with drugs, alcohol, sleep, or death. Within us there is a constant fight between the desire to extinguish self-consciousness and the drive to perpetuate the evolutionary process, which leads on to further enlightenment, openness, awareness, and pain. This conflict is perhaps as strong in our culture today as it has ever been.

We are constantly torn between dominance and submission. The book of Genesis reports that the Lord commanded us to "fill the earth and subdue it; and have dominion . . . over every living thing that moves upon the earth." Yet we know that we must submit to the processes of nature. Sin lies in the struggle between the necessary domination and the necessary submission. We are torn between the now and the future. The scientist in us may demonstrate that natural resources must be preserved for the future, but the breadwinner says we must eat *today,* which often means exploiting resources. Ambition, exuberance, and self-consciousness declaim that as much as possible has to be seized right away—"The moment is now!" —but other voices whisper, "You can't take it with you." We are forever embroiled in conflicts of this kind.

Thus, sin is of the spirit. It is indigenous to the spirit. It belongs to the spirit. Without it, there would be no spirit—not as we know man, not as we know spirit. I have indicated that one of our temptations is to avoid the human dilemma. If we could find some way to avoid it, we could eliminate much of the confusion and turmoil of conflicting inheritances. But as long as we do not transcend the human state, and as long as we are still striving animals, we will be embroiled in sin. It is a deep, ineradicable part of us.

Sin at the spiritual level must not be confused with the errors we make in eating or in drinking, with the kinds of books we read or movies we see, with sexual relationships and desires, with work choices, or with the rules of society. The latter are the traditional simple ways of thinking about sin. They diminish its grandeur, domesticate it, and so make it manageable. This serves to put the control of sin into the hands of ecclesiastics and public officials who can write rules about it and control it by dictating what we do or see, how we should entertain, or how we should express ourselves. At the same time they use the punishment of sin as a further means of ecclesiastic or social control. Sin is reduced to human error, and sinlessness becomes a matter of social organization or of will.

It was for such reasons that Jesus was so hard on the Pharisees because of their righteousness. Laws may be a satisfactory achievement from a government standpoint, but as Paul, Jesus, and all the prophets knew, laws are not adequate. Indeed, the more rules we have, the greater our capability of finding ways around them and coming out pious and complacent over our goodness and achievement. So, said Jesus to the Pharisees, you are like whited sepulchers; you look good in the social performance, but inside, there is nothing but death. He warned: "You tithe mint and dill and cummin, and have neglected the weightier matters of the law, justice and mercy and faith; these you ought to have done, without neglecting the others. You blind guides, straining out a gnat and swallowing a camel!" (Matt. 23:23.) Though many religious persons have appreciated this distinction, organized religion has flourished on the propagation of rules and procedures that could be used to dominate and control. Sin must not be reduced to that level.

The great leaders of Christianity all knew this. They understood that sin was a deep stain on the nature of man. (My nomenclature is different in that I call sin a quality of man's goodness, not a stain, but we agree on its significance.) They recognized that sin was not trivial. Limited as they were in scientific understanding, they realized that sin was deep in man and potentially self-defeating. The Biblical story is elegant testimony: Sin was put in the beginning, dramatized as an act of disobedience against God by the eating of the fruit of the tree of knowledge. In other words, as soon as man became aware of himself—which is to say as soon as he became man—he entered into sin. So deep was his sin, in fact, that he could never get rid of it by himself. The first Adam, supernaturally created, brought the punishment of exclusion from the garden, and only the Second Adam, also supernaturally created, could relieve him of his sin.

But while we can agree with the early Christians on the intrinsic nature of sin, we cannot accept their solution to the problem without betraying our enormous advantages of fact, insight, and understanding. The traditional Christian solution is what I call the "hero substitute." We look to someone else, someone greater than we—an anthropomorphic God—to save us from our sins because we cannot do it ourselves. When civilization was younger, this solution was tolerable, but it is not today. No one blames a child for running to its parents for help, but the time comes when childhood is outgrown and the person waits at his or her own peril for Mother or Dad to come to the rescue. Sheldon Kopp expresses the idea beautifully: "There are no fathers or mothers for grown-ups, only brothers or sisters."[38] Surely we are mature enough now to understand that there *is* no savior waiting in the wings to release us from sin.

Even in Christian dogma there is no claim that the supernatural solution will save us from the turmoil of human existence. The ultimate reward is cast off into a future heavenly realm. But while we live here on earth, we do not escape the burden of living in confusion, contradiction, and sin.

Living with Sin

If, as I have maintained, the responsibility is squarely on *our* shoulders to cope with sin, how are we to do it? I shall present what I like to call the religious answer. It is tempting to call it the new religious answer, for it is quite different from the customary, conventional, orthodox Christian approach—but it is not really new. Sensitive, understanding humanists who have appreciated the nature of a nonpersonal God have always accepted this kind of answer. It has its roots in the Judeo-Christian tradition but is more strongly expressed in Buddhism, Taoism, and Zen.

First, we must learn to accept the eternal conflict. Whether we believe in that future heavenly escape or not, as long as we are part of mankind we will find no way around the conflict. It is between ourselves and others, our pasts and our futures, our minds and our bodies, our selfishness and our generosity, our violence and our love, our private lives and our work lives, our desires and our capacities. We should accept these conflicts not begrudgingly but wholeheartedly and lovingly, for they are part of our genius.

Second, we must, as the prophet Micah commanded, "love mercy and kindness." Knowing our eternal conflicts, appreciating our human failings, recognizing our shame at not being what we want to be, realizing how often we betray our creative possibilities for the recessive security and comfort of the establishment, we must love mercy and kindness because we need them. This means that if our brother fails himself, us, or our community once, twice, ten times, or a hundred times, we must go on forgiving, because we know that we are all subject and vulnerable to sin. We too must go on sinning.

There is a beautiful episode in the play *Green Pastures*. God comes down to walk the earth to find out what's happening to his children. He finds that one of the defenders of the city of Jerusalem, which is being besieged by the Romans, is a believer in a new God of mercy. Disguised as a backcountry preacher, the Lord says: "What do you mean, a God of mercy? Don't you worship the Lord God Jehovah any more?"

The defender answers, "Oh, no, we don't worship that old God of wrath and vengeance any more, we worship the Lord God of Hosea."

"What kind of a God is he?" the Lord asks.

"Well, he is a God of mercy."

"Oh," says God, "where did your Hosea learn that?"

The defender answers, "Why, the same way anyone ever learns it—through suffering."

Through our suffering we learn about a God of mercy—through our shames, sorrows, and regrets as well as through our physical infirmities. We learn to offer mercy to each other because we need it in order to prevail.

Mercy and kindness do not mean that discipline must be thrown to the winds. When Jesus forgave the woman who had been taken in adultery, he did not intend to abolish the law and its penalties. There were no extenuating circumstances presented for that woman—it was a flagrant case. Many hundreds of Jewish women had been stoned to death for adultery, and many more would be in the future. He forgave because he could. Mercy is an ideal. It cannot be weighed and measured and balanced and counted. It must always be free and unearned and undeserved. The law, business, and government with their usual penalties, incentives, and routines go on, for they are necessary too. They are the only way in which imperfect, self-centered persons like ourselves can possibly make it together. Mercy is a different and opposing principle that coexists with discipline and punishment. It seems as if life is impossible without laws and penalties, but it is equally clear that we cannot have justice without mercy. Mercy does not transcend justice. It makes justice. It is the essence of our humanity, for it is the recognition of our universal, inescapable sinful nature.

Third, we need to form and encourage religious communities. As I think of it, a religious community is made up of people who care for one another in particular and for mankind in general, who understand the need for mercy and therefore strive to support, inspire, encourage, and accept one another.

The religious community should be a place where the one who has the worst opinion of himself or herself can be accepted. There will be fortunate, blessed people in that community, but they will realize that they are no better than the miserable, unfortunate ones. They will be aware that their good fortune is due in large part to circumstances they themselves did not create, such as friends and family who gave them love and kindness early in life, or good health, or extraordinary talents. Status through achievement will not be important in such a community; a person will be valued because he or she *is* or *cares,* not because of what he or she has done.

Such a religious community would have no secular power, it would not be dedicated to community-improvement projects, it would not seek to proselytize. But it would play an indispensable role in the development of spiritual understanding, individuality, and ability to cope with sin. It would recognize that we cannot do it alone. We must be with others who are trying to understand. We must be with others who seek the courage to be themselves, with their hidden strengths and aspirations as well as with their hidden weaknesses and guilts. We will not find help in acquiring that courage in the competition of business or a profession, or at cocktail parties, or in the locker room. For the world does not reward our hearts, our being, our selfhood; it rewards our achievements. I look to the religious community as one place where we can talk in candor about our sinfulness, where we can go into the deep recesses of ourselves and pull out the dirty, ugly, mean, unkind, socially unacceptable thoughts and motivations—dredge them up from the pits in our dreams, unashamed and unafraid. They are part of our being, along with our loves and creativity, like the Yin and the Yang.

The church is—or should be—the stimulus for the religious community. The church group, as I see it, would have much the same function as the "Group" that Erich Fromm envisions. According to Fromm:

> The Groups would develop a new style of life, unsentimental, realistic, honest, courageous, and active. It must be stressed that realistic unsentimentality—bordering, if you like, on cynicism—needs to be united with deep faith and hope. Usually the two are disconnected. People of faith and hope are often unrealistic, and the realists have little faith or hope. We shall find a way out of the present situation only if realism and faith become blended again as they were in some of the great teachers of mankind.
>
> The members of the Group would speak a new language which expresses rather than obscures, the language of a man who is the subject of his activities, not the alienated master of things which he manages in the category of "having" or "using." They would have a different style of consumption, not necessarily the minimum, but a meaningful consumption, one that serves the needs of life, not the needs of the producers. They would attempt to achieve personal change. Becoming vulnerable, active, they would practice contemplation, meditation, the art of

being quiet, undriven, and ungreedy; in order to understand the world around them, they would try to understand the forces within themselves which motivate them. They would try to transcend their "ego" and to be "open" to the world. They would try to rely on their own thinking and feeling, to make their own judgments and take their chances; they would try to achieve an optimum of freedom, that is, of real independence, and give up the worship of and fixation on idols of any kind. They would overcome the incestuous ties to the past, to where they came from, to family and land, and replace them by a loving and critical concern. They would develop the fearlessness which only deeprootedness in oneself, conviction, and a full relatedness to the world can give.[39]

Fourth, we need to learn more about how to manage sin. At best, our efforts will be bumbling, but we can at least work in the right direction and with guidelines that are valid and scientifically sound in the light of modern knowledge.

I suggest that we begin with the symbol of the cross. As indicated earlier, I do not accept the supernatural sanction of the hero who died to save us from our sins. That interpretation of the crucifixion is outmoded for most people. But there is a glory in the cross that makes it a valid symbol now, perhaps even more relevant today than in centuries past. The meaning of the cross is that we must be broken in order to understand our sins and failures. Or, to put it more positively, we must be broken in order to appreciate the unlimited possibilities of growth in the goodness of God, in loving relationships. No matter where we are or how advanced, we are only a step on the way. The future lies infinitely in front of us, but our patterns and establishments must be broken if we are to move on to new forms and new ways.

The cross is a way of foreclosing our claims to

righteousness, dispelling our feelings of smug self-satisfaction, cutting down our arrogance. The cross shatters idolatry. It says that no matter how good we are, there is a greater good. No matter how great and good the end we seek, there are greater goods. We always tend to settle on the good we know and to worship it. Our favorite heroes, beliefs, and institutions assume the role of the ultimate and become as God. The cross says *no* to all of this. It says that there are greater goods than any now known. It says that there will always be better ways opening up for the questing heart and mind.

No matter how fine our ways, they are not good enough. No matter how well they suit us, they are inadequate for future growth and understanding. At best, they are only tools. So there is nothing we have or cherish that cannot be lost, altered, or replaced. Our religious beliefs, our moral codes, our organizations, structures, and systems, our sciences, our loves, our individual and national hopes—all stand in need of being broken in behalf of transforming growth.

Man should at no time assume that the infinite possibilities of God have been realized. If God is creativity itself, we must constantly be opening up to the greater process, constantly moving on to the better organization, the greater hope, the finer ideal, the more releasing and supportive morality. It is not enough that the hero, the Savior, the Lord, and the Enlightened One experience the cross. This must be the experience of each of us. Such growth is the way of salvation. It is the strange solution of religion to the eternal dilemma of the animal seeking to become God. It is the way to true humanity.

NOTES

1. Lewis Mumford, *The Pentagon of Power* (Harcourt Brace Jovanovich, Inc., 1970), p. 54.

2. The Yin and Yang symbol has been used for years by the Fountain Club of Fountain Street Church and is on display in the chapel. The symbol is also incorporated in the jacket design of this book.

3. James Stephens, *A Singing Wind* (The Macmillan Company, 1968).

4. Quoted in Karl Menninger, *Crime of Punishment* (The Viking Press, 1968), p. 164.

5. Quoted in Rollo May, *Love and Will* (W. W. Norton & Company, Inc., 1969), p. 145.

6. May, *Love and Will,* p. 165.

7. Quoted in J. Bronowski, *The Faces of Violence* (George Braziller, Inc., 1955), p. 22.

8. Carl G. Jung, *Memories, Dreams, Reflections* (Pantheon Books, Inc., 1961), pp. 91–92.

9. Robert Frost, "America Is Hard to See," *In the Clearing* (Holt, Rinehart & Winston, Inc., 1962), p. 22.

10. See Dee Brown, *Bury My Heart at Wounded Knee* (Holt, Rinehart and Winston, Inc., 1971). For an illuminating

discussion of other destructive attitudes in our past and present, see Konrad Lorenz, *Civilized Man's Eight Deadly Sins* (Harcourt Brace Jovanovich, Inc., 1974). Lorenz concentrates on the following problems: overpopulation, devastation of the natural environment, competitiveness, entropy of feeling, genetic decay, the break with tradition, the easy indoctrinability of modern man, and willingness to manufacture and use nuclear weapons.

11. Jonas Salk, *The Survival of the Wisest* (Harper & Row, Publishers, Inc., 1973), p. 71.

12. Aleksandr I. Solzhenitsyn, *The Gulag Archipelago 1918–1956* (Harper & Row, Publishers, Inc., 1974), pp. 591–592.

13. Whitney J. Oates and Eugene O'Neill, Jr. (eds.), *The Complete Greek Drama* (Random House, Inc., 1938), Vol. I, p. 194.

14. Joshua Loth Liebman, *Peace of Mind* (Simon & Schuster, Inc., 1946), pp. 38–39.

15. Joseph Barry, *Passions and Politics* (Doubleday & Company, Inc., 1972), p. 364.

16. *The New York Times,* March 30, 1974.

17. Aleksandr I. Solzhenitzyn, *The Nobel Lecture on Literature, 1972* (Harper & Row, Publishers, Inc., 1972), pp. 25–26.

18. Erich Fromm, *The Heart of Man* (Harper & Row, Publishers, Inc., 1964,) p. 42.

19. *Ibid.,* p. 28.

20. R. D. Laing, *The Politics of Experience* (Pantheon Bks., Inc., 1967), p. 36.

21. *The New York Times,* Oct. 20, 1971, p. 49.

22. Ramsey Clark, *Crime in America* (Simon & Schuster, Inc., 1970), p. 314.

23. Marshall McLuhan, *Understanding Media* (McGraw-Hill Book Co., Inc., 1961), p. 186.

24. T. S. Eliot, "Little Gidding," "Four Quartets," *Complete Poems and Plays, 1909–1950* (Harcourt, Brace and Company, Inc., 1952), p. 142.

25. May, *Love and Will,* p. 111.

26. Arthur Janov, *The Primal Scream* (Dell Pub. Co., Inc., 1970), p. 23.

27. Francis W. Bourdillon, "The Night Has a Thousand Eyes," in John Bartlett, *Familiar Quotations* (Little, Brown & Company, 1968), p. 826.

28. Karl Menninger, *The Vital Balance* (The Viking Press, 1963), p. 375.

29. Abraham Maslow, *Toward a Psychology of Being* (D. Van Nostrand Company, Inc., 1968), p. 142.

30. Viktor E. Frankl, *Man's Search for Meaning* (Washington Square Press, 1963), pp. 117–118.

31. H. G. Wells, *The Croquet Player* (The Viking Press, Inc., 1936).

32. Aldous Huxley, *Brave New World* (Harper & Brothers, 1932).

33. Archibald Cox, "Ends," *The New York Times Magazine,* May 19, 1974, p. 66.

34. Henri Charrier, *Papillon* (Pocket Book, Inc., 1971), p. 396.

35. Quoted inside the front cover of *Your Land, Your Jeep, and You,* by Ed Zern (American Motors Corporation, 1972).

36. Albert Einstein, *The New York Times,* March 29, 1972, p. 22.

37. Nikos Kazantzakis, *The Saviors of God* (Simon & Schuster, Inc., 1960), p. 74.

38. Sheldon Kopp, *If You Meet the Buddha on the Road, Kill Him!* (Palo Alto, California: Science and Behavior Bks., Inc., 1972), p. 140.

39. Erich Fromm, *The Revolution of Hope* (Harper & Row, Publishers, Inc., 1968), p. 159.

INDEX